NEW DIRECTIONS FOR STUDENT SERVICES

Margaret J. Barr, *Northwestern University*
EDITOR-IN-CHIEF

M. Lee Upcraft, *The Pennsylvania State University*
ASSOCIATE EDITOR

Student Services in a Changing Federal Climate

Michael D. Coomes
Bowling Green State University

Donald D. Gehring
Bowling Green State University

EDITORS

Number 68, Winter 1994

JOSSEY-BASS PUBLISHERS
San Francisco

STUDENT SERVICES IN A CHANGING FEDERAL CLIMATE
Michael D. Coomes, Donald D. Gehring (eds.)
New Directions for Student Services, no. 68
Margaret J. Barr, Editor-in-Chief
M. Lee Upcraft, Associate Editor

Microfilm copies of issues and articles are available in 16mm and 35mm,
as well as microfiche in 105mm, through University Microfilms Inc., 300
North Zeeb Road, Ann Arbor, Michigan 48106-1346.

LC 85-644751   ISSN 0164-7970   ISBN 0-7879-9997-0

NEW DIRECTIONS FOR STUDENT SERVICES is part of The Jossey-Bass Higher
and Adult Education Series and is published quarterly by Jossey-Bass Inc.,
Publishers, 350 Sansome Street, San Francisco, California 94104-1342.
Second-class postage paid at San Francisco, California, and at additional
mailing offices. POSTMASTER: Send address changes to New Directions for
Teaching and Learning, Jossey-Bass Inc., Publishers, 350 Sansome Street,
San Francisco, California 94104-1342.

SUBSCRIPTIONS for 1994 cost $47.00 for individuals and $62.00 for institutions, agencies, and libraries.

EDITORIAL CORRESPONDENCE should be sent to the Editor-in-Chief,
Margaret J. Barr, 633 Clark Street, 2-219, Evanston, Illinois 60208-1103.

Cover photograph by Wernher Krutein/PHOTOVAULT © 1990.

Manufactured in the United States of America. Nearly all Jossey-Bass
books, jackets, and periodicals are printed on recycled paper that contains
at least 50 percent recycled waste, including 10 percent postconsumer
waste. Many of our materials are also printed with vegetable-based inks;
during the printing process, these inks emit fewer volatile organic com-
pounds (VOCs) than petroleum-based inks. VOCs contribute to the formation of smog.

CONTENTS

EDITORS' NOTES

Although the federal government's relationship to higher education can be traced to the Northwest Ordinance of 1787, extensive federal involvement in higher education is a relatively recent phenomenon. Starting with the GI bills following World War II and the Korean War, and moving through the civil rights and student aid legislation of the Johnson years, the federal government has become increasingly active in developing policy that directly affects college campuses. Today the federal government has become one of the most important constituents of campus student affairs administrators. Student affairs practitioners are no longer able to direct their attention solely to their campuses. They cannot limit themselves to the day-to-day operation of their office, to meetings with students, fellow administrators, and faculty, and to shaping and directing policy that directs the lives of students. The diligent student affairs administrator must now stay abreast of numerous federal laws and regulations to ensure that barriers to higher education are removed for a wide class of students, that institutions are honest and open in sharing information about the college experience with current and prospective students, and that members of the campus community are educated about the dangers of drugs, alcohol abuse, and sexual assaults. The government has become a significant player in the creation of policy for individual campuses and student affairs administrators must understand the policy process in order to be able to influence it.

This sourcebook is intended to help student affairs administrators understand the nature of federal intervention in the operation of student services. A secondary purpose is to provide student affairs administrators with enough information about the federal policy process that they will be empowered to consider influencing the process. Federal legislation and administrative rules are not created in a closed system. Student affairs administrators have ample opportunities to shape the decision-making processes that result in the creation of new laws and the interpretation of existing ones. If they understand the process more clearly, administrators can begin to exercise their rights to shape policies that may not be in the best interests of their institution's and the nation's students.

This sourcebook is intended for several audiences. Campus administrators will find it a useful source of information on federal program participation and legal responsibility. Faculty members in student affairs and higher education programs will find it a useful addition to the limited resources on federal involvement in higher education and, most specifically, in student affairs administration. Graduate students will be able to use the sourcebook for ideas for additional research projects and dissertations.

Two caveats are needed. In an effort to make the work readable and to avoid duplication of information, we have not included the public law numbers for the various pieces of legislation cited by the sourcebook's authors. For readers who may wish to locate and read the original legislation referenced in the sourcebook, we have included a listing of all pertinent legislation with their public law numbers in the Appendix. In addition, the information in this sourcebook does not constitute legal advice. It is provided only to assist the reader to understand better the parameters of federal involvement in higher education.

In the first chapter Michael D. Coomes provides a context for subsequent chapters by tracing the development of federal involvement in higher education. He begins with the ratification of the Survey Ordinance of 1785 and goes through the passage of the National and Community Service Trust Act of 1993. Special attention is paid to legislation that has had a direct impact on the ability of campuses to provide service to students. Pertinent legislation includes the National Defense Education Act, the Higher Education Act of 1965, the Family Educational Rights and Privacy Act, and the Americans with Disabilities Act. Themes explored include the justification for federal involvement in higher education; the changing rationale for that involvement; and increased federal intervention and decreased campus autonomy.

The second chapter, by Coomes and Donald Hossler, provides an overview of the federal policy making process. Discussion focuses on the definition and purpose of policy, the way policy is formulated and implemented, and the various branches of federal government involved in policy making. The chapter addresses such issues as the policy-making context, the philosophical reasons for creating federal policy, and the participants in the process.

The third chapter, by Timothy A. Bills and Patrick J. Hall, examines federal legislation designed to combat various forms of discrimination occurring on college campuses and in society at large. Attention is given to legislation and court rulings aimed at increasing the level of diversity on campus. The chapter emphasizes the need for administrators to be aware of their legal obligations to make their campuses more accessible and less hostile to an increasingly diverse student clientele. In the fourth chapter, Donald D. Gehring continues the discussion of the primary laws affecting the administration of student affairs. Gehring focuses his discussion on protective policy laws that are intended to address a wide range of current campus issues, such as campus security, consumer information, and alcohol and drug use. As is the case in Chapter Three, applicable case law interpreting the statutes is also discussed.

Chapter Five, by John H. Schuh and Tracy Y. Ogle, moves the focus away from the federal government and toward the campus. Schuh and Ogle present strategies for implementing various federal policies from the perspective of the campus administrator. Their discussion focuses on a range of issues, including understanding the requirements of federal law and administrative regulation, forming partnerships, and developing resources for guidance and instruction in meeting federal policy requirements.

In Chapter Five, Gehring suggests that although federal intervention has been directed toward laudable goals, the intervention itself may be unlawful. That intervention, coupled with an overly complicated and intrusive regulatory process, has caused both a loss of trust and an adversarial relationship to develop between higher education and the federal government. Strategies for responding to the government are provided.

The concluding chapter, by Coomes and Gehring, presents an annotated list of resources that should be of interest to student affairs practitioners who wish to learn more about federal policy making and the role of the government in directing student affairs policy. Resources cover such topics as policy analyses focusing on student affairs related subjects, the policy process, legal issues, and legislative affairs.

Michael D. Coomes
Donald D. Gehring
Editors

MICHAEL D. COOMES *is assistant professor of higher education and student affairs at Bowling Green State University. Before holding that position, he served as the director of financial aid at Seattle University and at Saint Martin's College. He is a member of the American College Personnel Association and the National Association of Student Personnel Administrators.*

DONALD D. GEHRING *is professor of higher education and student affairs and director of the higher education doctoral program at Bowling Green State University. His primary research activities center on legal issues in higher education. His books include* The College Student and the Courts *with D. P. Young (1977) and* Administering College and University Housing: A Legal Perspective *with others (1988). In 1991 Gehring was named a senior scholar by the American College Personnel Association.*

This chapter examines the development of federal efforts that have shaped the interaction between colleges and students. A historical overview is offered and major themes are explored.

A History of Federal Involvement in the Lives of Students

Michael D. Coomes

> I hope, believe, and dream that national service will remain throughout the life of America not a series of promises but a series of challenges across all the generations and all walks of life to help us to rebuild our troubled but wonderful land. I hope that some day the success of this program will make it possible for every young American who wishes to serve and earn credit against a college education or other kinds of education and training to do that. And I believe it will happen.
> —President William J. Clinton (1993, pp. 1823–1824)

On September 21, 1993, President Clinton offered these comments at a ceremony to mark the signing of the National and Community Service Trust Act of 1993. The creation of a new set of community service opportunities and their connection to funding for higher education attendance marked the most recent chapter in federal involvement in higher education. Like many pieces of legislation, the National and Community Service Trust Act of 1993, while it has a significant impact on higher education, is really intended to realize other goals—in this case the creation of organizations and opportunities to foster community service. As a secondary outcome, this kind of legislation benefits postsecondary institutions and students.

The lack of a clear and consistent federal philosophy of intervention in higher education is the result of constitutional constraints and historical happenstance. Article X of the U.S. Constitution states, "The powers not delegated to the United States by the Constitution, nor prohibited by it to the States, are reserved to the States respectively, or to the people." One of the powers not covered by the Constitution is education and as such it is a "power reserved to the States . . . or to the people." The federal government's role in higher education has evolved over the course of the past 210 years, from limited involvement, as mandated by the Constitution, to the significant involvement we know today. The evolution of that involvement and the changing nature of the interaction between the federal government and higher education will be outlined in this chapter.

One limitation of this presentation should be noted. Although there has been a wide range of federal institutional interventions (for example, faculty development, libraries, research support) this chapter will focus on federal interventions targeted at students.

Early Federal Initiatives: Institution Building and Development

The earliest intervention by the national government in higher education predates the ratification of the Constitution by two years. The Survey Ordinance of 1785 required newly created townships in the Western Territory to set aside one section of land for the endowment of schools and seminaries ("Federal Education Programs . . . ," 1965). Similarly, the Northwest Ordinance of 1787 provided for the creation of seminaries of learning because "religion, morality, and knowledge being necessary to good government and the happiness of mankind, schools and the means of education shall forever be encouraged" (Commager, 1958, p. 131). Both of these pieces of legislation left the creation of what would eventually become colleges to the local citizenry.

The federal government became directly involved in the creation of colleges with the founding of the military academy at West Point, New York, in 1802 and the naval academy at Annapolis, Maryland, in 1845. The creation of the service academies represents the "extent of the federal government's direct management of institutions" (Gladieux and Wolanin, 1976, p. 3). However, their creation was not intended as a means for involving the federal government in higher education; rather it was seen as a way to ensure the development of a skilled and trained officer corps.

Providing federal land for the development of colleges became widespread with the passage of the Morrill Land Grant Acts. In an attempt to harness science to the plow, Congress passed the first of Justin Morrill's acts in 1862 (Brubacher and Rudy, 1976; Rudolph, 1990). This legislation authorized "grants of federal land to each state for the establishment of colleges specializing in agricultural and mechanical arts" ("Federal Education Programs . . . ," 1965, p. 1196). In order to avoid the appearance of violating Article X, the creation of higher education institutions was tied to land development (Finn, 1978). As Gladieux and Wolanin (1976) conclude, "Thus support for higher education was indistinguishable from federal support for road construction or river and harbor improvements. The object of each case was to make public lands more attractive to prospective buyers" (p. 5).

In 1890, a second Morrill Act was passed by Congress. This act came in response to the difficult financial conditions that many of the colleges that had been created by the first act were facing. The Morrill Act of 1890 provided annual federal funds to the states for their land grant colleges. However, and more importantly, the act aided in the creation of land grant colleges to educate the new freedmen in the southern and border states. The first "Negro Land Grant College was not created until 1871. At that time, the State of Mississippi granted three-fifths of the benefit from the land sales to establish Alcorn University" ("The Unique Role and Mission . . . ," 1988, p. 12). Following the establishment of Alcorn University, South Carolina provided funds from the sale of lands to a private institution, Claflin College, to fulfill the land grant function for that state. Virginia was the only other state to take advantage of the original land grant law to aid education for African Americans. In 1872 funds from the sale of lands were provided to Hampton Institute; later Virginia created Virginia State College, a separate African American land grant college ("The Unique Role and Mission . . . ," 1988). Thus, as a vehicle for creating educational opportunities for African Americans, the first Morrill Act was not particularly successful. Much of its failure can be attributed to state legislatures, which had the responsibility for allocating funds for education and which did not perceive the education of African Americans to be important or necessary ("The Unique Role and Mission . . . ," 1988). The second act attempted to address this shortcoming by "the provision in the bill which stipulated that annual grants be withheld from states which segregated blacks without providing separate agricultural and mechanical colleges for them" (Fleming, 1976, p. 70). If the first act provided few incentives for states to develop educational opportunities for African Americans, the second gave them de jure reasons for supporting segregation. The second Morrill Act's "separate but equal" provision satisfied the legislatures of many southern and border states that, before 1890, had been unwilling to invest in the creation of colleges for African Americans. Following passage of the second Morrill Act, seventeen states created land grant colleges for them. However, in reality, educational opportunities offered by these newly created agricultural and mechanical colleges were never equal to those offered by white land grant colleges ("The Unique Role and Mission . . . ," 1988). For additional insight into the development of higher education opportunities for African Americans and the impact of the Morrill Land Grant Acts on the development of historically black colleges, the reader is directed to Fleming (1976).

For a variety of reasons—land development, support of the sciences, agricultural training, and the education of African Americans—the Morrill Acts had a profound impact on higher education. The nation's land grant colleges represent an important national resource. In 1992 alone, the institutional members of the National Association of State Universities and Land Grant Colleges (NASULGC), many of which are land grant colleges, enrolled 2,750,556 students. Further, NASULGC annually awards "about one-third of all bachelor's and master's degrees, 60 percent of all U.S. doctoral degrees, and

70 percent of the nation's engineering degrees" (National Association of State Universities and Land Grant Colleges, 1994, p. 6). As Brubacher and Rudy (1976) note, "The Morrill Act was significant because it initiated the practice of using federal grants-in-aid to achieve specific objectives desired by government. This was to prove a powerful weapon during subsequent years in developing various federally controlled programs for the 'general welfare.' The act introduced also the principle of equalization of opportunity, a concept which was to become normative for most federal legislation dealing with education in the twentieth century" (p. 228).

In the period following the passage of the Morrill Acts, the locus of federal involvement in higher education shifted from Congress to the courts. In 1896, the Supreme Court, in *Plessy v. Ferguson,* validated the "separate but equal" doctrine outlined in the 1890 Morrill Act and ensured that educational opportunities for African Americans from elementary school through college would be limited. The *Plessy v. Ferguson* case dealt with the rights of African Americans to seek equal protection under the Thirteenth and Fourteenth Amendments (Fleming, 1976). The suit was brought by Homer Adolph Plessy, who was arrested for refusing to ride in the "colored" car of a train during a trip in Louisiana. Plessy charged that the 1890 Louisiana statute supporting separate but equal accommodations for the races was unconstitutional (Fleming, 1976). The Supreme Court sided with the state of Louisiana, ruling that "the Fourteenth Amendment did not intend 'to enforce absolute equality of the two races before the law, and to enforce commingling of the two races,' and it could not have eliminated distinctions upon race" (Fleming, 1976, p. 65).

The outcome of *Plessy v. Ferguson* was that education for African Americans would be accorded second-class status in the United States. For higher education, this generally meant devoting far fewer resources to southern black land grant colleges and closing the doors of many publicly supported southern institutions to African Americans. As Fleming (1976) points out, "Not since the abolition of slavery had a decision made such a severe and negative impact on black education. Taking their cue from the *Plessy* decision, southern states, using the sanction of law, began to impose a series of political, civic, economic, and social restrictions on blacks. State after state rewrote its constitution and implemented statutes to legally formalize patterns of segregation and discrimination" (p. 66).

The 1930s and 1940s: Emphasis on Students

From the turn of the century until the Great Depression, colleges grew in number and enrollment at a steady pace, and federal involvement in higher education was limited. The U.S. Coast Guard Academy was created in 1900. During World War I, the "Students Army Training Corps was set up 'to prevent unnecessary and wasteful depletion of the colleges' " (Brubacher and Rudy, 1976, p. 225). More extensive federal involvement in all aspects of

American life, including higher education, was to come during the administration of Franklin D. Roosevelt.

In an attempt to pull the United States out of the Great Depression, which began in 1929, the Roosevelt administration implemented a number of public works programs (for example, Civilian Conservation Corps, Works Progress Administration). One of these programs, the National Youth Administration (NYA), became the first major program of direct assistance to students. From 1935 to 1943, the federal government spent over $93 million and employed 620,000 students in the NYA. Like much of the higher education legislation that preceded and would follow it, the NYA was prompted by a noneducational policy issue—the need to provide work during the depression—rather than a desire to provide aid to institutions or students (Brubacher and Rudy, 1976). As a program of direct aid to students intended to serve multiple goals, the NYA became the precursor of the most ambitious program of federal involvement in higher education, the Serviceman's Readjustment Act of 1944.

The Serviceman's Readjustment Act (the GI Bill of Rights) became the largest program of direct aid to students and it profoundly shaped the face of higher education. The GI Bill was enacted for two purposes: to reward the veterans of the Second World War for their service and to ease the burden on a fragile economy that a substantial increase in the number of employable men and women would represent (Rivlin, 1961). Through a series of direct grants to students and, initially, subsidies to institutions, the GI Bill represented a significant infusion of resources into higher education. As a result of the bill, tens of thousands of veterans entered college (Fenske, 1983). Further, because many of them were first-generation college students, they placed new demands on the colleges they attended. They were vocationally minded, frequently married, and not very interested in the social aspects of higher education. These new students "created a tremendous need for academic, personal, and financial advising on nearly every campus in the country . . . and breathed new life into student-oriented services of all kinds" (Fenske, 1989b, p. 34).

The 1930s and 1940s marked both the emergence of the United States as an international power and an expansion of the federal role in the lives of Americans. This expansion included increased intervention in higher education. The focus on students, through programs like the National Youth Administration and the Serviceman's Readjustment Act, set a precedent for the focus on students that would emerge in the early 1970s.

In 1946, President Harry Truman appointed a commission to " 'reexamine our system of higher education in terms of its objectives, methods, and facilities and in light of the social role it has to play' " (Brubacher and Rudy, 1976, p. 234). The six-volume report of the Truman commission, entitled *Higher Education for American Democracy* (1947), was to have an intense impact on federal intervention in higher education for the next twenty years. At its heart, the report called for an increased role for the federal government in assuring that higher education was open to all. To this end it stated,

> The American people should set as their ultimate goal an educational system in which at no level—high school, college, graduate school, or professional school—will a qualified individual in any part of the country encounter an insuperable economic barrier to the attainment of the kind of education suited to his aptitudes and interests.
>
> This means we shall aim at making higher education equally available to all young people . . . to the extent that their capacity warrants a further social investment in their training [*Higher Education for American Democracy,* 1947, p. 36].

The Truman commission set as the fulfillment of this goal the doubling of postsecondary enrollments by the end of the following decade. To facilitate such a significant expansion, the commission offered a number of important programmatic and institutional recommendations, including the following:

1. An expansion of free public education to include two years beyond high school. All the states were encouraged to establish community colleges that would be part of the public education system, accessible to all potential students, and free of charge.
2. The creation of a federally funded scholarship program that would aid non-veteran students.
3. A program of federal grants for public institutions for capital expenses.
4. A call for legislation that would eliminate racial and religious discrimination in the selection of college students [Brubacher and Rudy, 1976].

The Truman commission recommendations were to have a significant impact on the shape and scope of higher education. Many of its goals would be realized during the 1950s and 1960s. The goal of doubling enrollments would be realized by 1967. Total college enrollment had stood at 2,338,226 in 1947, the year the Truman commission report was published; by 1967 total college enrollment had risen to 6,911,748 students (Snyder and Hoffman, 1993). New student aid programs would be created in the late 1950s and early 1960s to realize the goal of expanded aid to all students, and significant federal resources were appropriated for capital improvements at both public and private institutions. Racial barriers to enrollment would begin to be dropped following the Supreme Court's landmark case *Brown v. Board of Education* (1954).

The 1950s and 1960s: Equalization of Opportunity

The federal government's movement to continue to promote equity that had begun with the Morrill Acts and continued with the GI bills of World War II and the Korean War saw its fulfillment in a series of court decisions and legislation in the 1950s and 1960s. The first of these, *Brown v. Board of Education,* which was initially directed at eliminating racial segregation in public elementary and secondary schools, was quickly extended to public colleges through decisions like *Florida ex rel. Hawkins v. Board of Control* (1956) (Kaplin, 1985). For a detailed accounting of the facts of *Brown* and the legal battles to bring a racial desegregation case to trial, the reader is directed to Kluger (1976). *Brown* and subsequent decisions legally banned racial segregation, but de facto segregation in public and private postsecondary institutions continued throughout the 1950s and 1960s. Additional impetus to open the college doors to all students came during the civil rights movement of the 1960s and culminated with the passage of the Civil Rights Act of 1964. Subsequent legislation (such as Title IX of the Education Amendments of 1972) provided legal protection for other students.

Another landmark case emanating from the civil rights movement, *Dixon v. Alabama State Board of Education* (1961), profoundly shaped the nature of the student institutional relationship. The case hinged on the issue of "whether [the] due process [clause of the Fourteenth Amendment] requires notice and some opportunity for hearing before students at a tax-supported college are expelled for misconduct" (Kaplin, 1985, p. 303). The case centered on Alabama State College's suspension of several African American students for participating in a lunch counter sit-in in Montgomery, Alabama. With the assistance of the National Association for the Advancement of Colored People and one of its young attorneys named Thurgood Marshall, the students sued the State Board of Education. They charged their rights to due process had been violated (the college had dismissed the students without recourse to a disciplinary hearing) and on appeal, the federal circuit court ruled in favor of the students. The court held that students at public institutions were covered by the Fourteenth Amendment and extended "due process safeguards available to students charged by college officials with misconduct" (Kaplin, 1985, p. 303). The practical implication of *Dixon* as well as other subsequent cases (for example, *Tinker v. Des Moines* [1969], *Healy v. James* [1972]) was the invalidation of the principle of in loco parentis as a legally tenable doctrine for guiding public colleges in their relationship with students. In loco parentis, the concept that colleges act on behalf of parents, had been validated by the courts in 1913, through their decision in the case of *Gott v. Berea College*. (Interestingly, the particulars of both *Gott* and *Dixon* were very similar; both cases stemmed from students' wishes to be served at restaurants near campus.) The principle of in loco parentis had served as the touchstone for student affairs practice and provided a philosophical justification for the student-institutional relationship (Fenske, 1989a). Court decisions like *Dixon* and *Tinker*, when coupled with the civil rights and women's movements, and the student activism of the 1960s, dealt a death blow to in loco parentis as a guiding philosophy for the student affairs profession, and forced the profession to look for a new philosophy to guide its practice.

The late 1950s and early 1960s saw a flurry of legislation that would for practical purposes realize many of the goals of the 1947 Truman Commission report. In 1950, Congress passed two important pieces of higher education legislation: the Housing Act, which authorized a fifty-year program of low interest loans to colleges for the construction of dormitories, and the National Science Foundation Act, which provided for the promotion of scientific research through programs of research grants to institutions and fellowships to graduate students studying science and mathematics ("Federal Education Programs . . . ," 1965). However, the most important legislation of the 1950s was the National Defense Education Act (NDEA) of 1958.

> [In the early 1950s] only education programs that could be billed as 'defense' measures—to meet a crisis or which aided education peripherally but were basically designed to meet another kind of problem, such as food surpluses or job shortages, or which responded to special pressures such as 'impacted areas' aid—received approval. These [programs,] to be sure, reached out to a large segment of the U.S. school and college population but were not regarded as 'general school aid.' ["Federal Education Programs . . . ," 1965, p. 1197]

NDEA was enacted in response to the launching of the Russian satellite *Sputnik* and to several reports outlining the nation's need for increased technical and scientific education. Although ostensibly a defense measure, the bill created a number of programs that would assist institutions and individual students. The centerpiece of the NDEA was the National Defense Student Loan program (currently the Federal Perkins Loan), the first program of generally available, federally funded, student aid. In addition to the creation of a student loan program, other higher education provisions of the NDEA included the following: (1) the creation of a graduate fellowship program that gave funding preference to those who wanted to teach at the college or university level; (2) the authorization of funds to assist colleges in the improvement of the teaching of modern foreign languages; (3) the creation of grants for the conduct of research on "innovative teaching aids" (Conlan, 1981, p. 18); and (4) the authorization of funds for the National Science Foundation to promote the dissemination of scientific information ("Federal Education Programs . . . ," 1965).

As King (1975) points out, the National Defense Education Act (NDEA) was important "not so much because of the specific provisions . . . but because of the psychological breakthrough it embodied. It asserted, more forcefully than at any time in nearly a century, a national interest in the quality of education that the states, communities, and private institutions provided" (p. 11). Conlan (1981) noted that, "Although the ostensible federal interest in passing the eclectic measure was national defense, there was also some suggestion that the federal government was moving in the direction of guaranteed opportunity for higher education" (p. 18). Another important outcome of NDEA was that the principal beneficiaries of federal education funding were students, not institutions. Although funds were routed through institutions, students were to be the recipients. The student versus institutional aid question, which was first raised with the passage of NDEA, would come to a head in 1972 when Congress debated reauthorizing the Higher Education Act of 1965.

The next important pieces of federal higher education legislation were enacted as part of Lyndon B. Johnson's Great Society ("Federal Education Programs . . . ," 1965; "Federal Education Programs," 1969). Many of the higher education programs that would be created as part of the Johnson initiatives were originally proposed by President John F. Kennedy in 1963. In his 1963 omnibus education package, Kennedy recommended the creation of an undergraduate scholarship program, a work study program, and a library aid program. Although student aid was an important part of the Kennedy education package, the only program Congress passed in 1963 was a bill providing building construction aid to colleges (Conlan, 1981).

"The years of President Johnson's administration are frequently referred to by college and university administrators as the 'golden years' for higher education in the post-World War II period. Certainly at no time before and at no time since has education, both higher and lower-school education, been as high on the national agenda of any administration" (Wilson, 1983, p. 49). President Johnson's interest in education was long-standing and deeply held. As a student at Southwest State Teacher's College, Johnson had struggled to make ends meet (Caro, 1982); as a teacher he had experienced the classroom firsthand; and as a member of Congress he had participated in the passage of the National Defense Education Act.

The first major piece of legislation sponsored by the Johnson administration that had an impact higher education was the Economic Opportunity Act of 1964. That act created the College Work Study Program, which was intended to create part-time jobs for needy students. The program was assigned to the Office of Educational Opportunity, where it remained until it was transferred to the Office of Education in 1965 (Moore, 1983).

Then, in 1965, Congress passed the Higher Education Act, by far the most comprehensive piece of higher education legislation to that time. Major provisions of the act included the creation of the Educational Opportunity Grant (EOG) program, a program of federally financed scholarships for low-income students; the creation of a program of guaranteed, subsidized loans; and the transfer of the College Work Study program from the Office of Economic Opportunity to the Office of Education. In addition to its student aid provisions, the act also established the Upward Bound program, a program intended to identify talented students who needed encouragement to pursue a college education, and the Teacher Corps, a program to improve the skills of experienced and novice teachers. The act also provided grants for university extension programs, provided aid to libraries, and authorized aid to developing institutions ("Federal Education Programs," 1969).

The Higher Education Act of 1965 was a landmark piece of higher education legislation passed in a watershed year for domestic social legislation. Other major legislation passed by Congress that year included Medicare, the Voting Rights Act, and the Elementary and Secondary School Act (Gladieux and Wolanin, 1976). All of this legislation had a similar purpose: increased access to social improvement programs. Increased access was a response to a felt need that Americans should not be denied access to agreed-upon social goods (for example, health care, education) because of their race or socio-economic status. The Higher Education Act "embodied for the first time an explicit commitment to equalizing college opportunities for needy students through grants and through programs such as Talent Search designed to facilitate access for the college-able poor" (Gladieux, 1983, p. 401).

The Higher Education Act added a scholarship program and a subsidized loan program to the existing financial aid programs thus building a comprehensive program of federal student assistance. With the addition of the Guaranteed Student Loan (GSL) program and the elimination of the "low-income" provision of the College Work Study program, HEA expanded student aid opportunities to middle-income students. The Higher Education Act fully laid the groundwork for federal involvement in student assistance and firmly established equal educational opportunity as a national educational policy preference.

The 1970s: Student Equity, Access, and Choice

The 1970s were characterized by legislation that was intended to extend educational opportunity to increased numbers of students and resulted in traditional-aged students being accorded adult status on college campuses. In 1971, the Twenty-sixth Amendment to the Constitution was ratified, lowering the voting age from 21 to 18 (Cultice, 1992; Kaplin, 1985) and according traditional-aged college students legal adulthood. Changing the age of majority required campuses to reconsider the legal status of students and influenced such issues as student-institutional contracts, voter registration and absentee ballot procedures, scheduling of elections, campaign canvassing and voter registration on campus, and reapportionment (Kaplin, 1985).

The next major federal initiative, the Education Amendments of 1972, continued the expansion of federal intervention in higher education. The congressional debates that led to the development and passage of the amendments broke down along two lines: whether student aid should be allocated in the form of institutional grants to combat the rising costs of instruction or whether it should come in the form of increased support for individual students (Gladieux and Wolanin, 1976). Valid arguments existed on both sides of the debate. Supporters of aid to students argued that student assistance avoided the constitutional questions of federal support for sectarian institutions by putting the funds in the hands of the consumers of higher education, and that it would improve quality through the imposition of free market mechanisms (Davis, 1972). Proponents of institutional aid suggested that a dominant student-aid approach could shift the burden of paying for college to students. The influx of federal funding, it was feared, would encourage institutions to increase costs and result in an inflationary spiral. In addition, those students who would not qualify for grant aid would be forced to carry large loan burdens or attend less expensive institutions. The primary supporter of aid to students was the new chairman of the Senate Labor and Education Committee, Claiborne Pell, who was particularly interested in making education a right for all students through a national entitlement program of direct grants. The chief advocate of aid to institutions was the influential chairperson of the House Special Education Subcommittee and chief architect of the Higher Education Act of 1965, Edith Green (D-OR), who pushed for an expansion of existing student aid programs to meet the needs of a growing college population coupled with a program of direct aid to institutions. After considerable debate and political maneuvering (the student aid programs contained in the final bill were somewhat lost in the contentious discussion of the use of forced busing to foster the integration of public elementary and secondary schools), the forces supporting direct aid to students won out and the Education Amendments of 1972 became law (Gladieux and Wolanin, 1976).

The Education Amendments of 1972 had a significant impact on the federal student aid programs and, through Title IX, on higher education in general ("Federal Education Programs," 1973). The most important provision of the Education Amendments of 1972 was the creation of the Basic Educational Opportunity Grant (BEOG) program (renamed Pell Grants in 1980 in honor of the program's original sponsor). The BEOG program was to be an "entitlement" program of grants for needy college students that was intended to serve as the foundation of the student's financial aid award. To placate supporters of institutional aid, funding for the BEOG program was tied to funding for the campus-based programs—Supplemental Grants, National Direct Student Loans, and College Work Study ("1972 Education Act . . . ," 1972). The legislation also extended and increased authorization for the campus-based programs; expanded eligibility for the GSL program to students from middle-income families; created the Student Loan Marketing Association (Sallie Mae), a secondary market and warehousing system for the Guaranteed Student Loan program; created, for the first time, a program of direct aid to institutions; and established the State Student Incentive Grant (SSIG) program ("Federal Education Programs," 1973; Moore, 1983).

Gladieux and Wolanin (1976) note that the Education Amendments of 1972 were "indeed a measure of staggering comprehensiveness, easily the longest federal education statute in history" (p. 230). In addition to its programmatic changes, the amendments produced a number of normative and philosophical changes. Primary among these was the decision to place purchasing power in the hands of students through the creation of the BEOG program. Although an institutional aid program was also created by P.L. 92–318, the program has never been funded. Aid to students, therefore, "has been established as the principal mechanism of federal support" for higher education (Gladieux and Wolanin, 1976, p. 225).

Educational opportunity as a right—a principle theme of the Higher Education Act of 1965—became "the central commitment of federal higher education policy" with the passage of the Education Amendments of 1972 (Gladieux and Wolanin, 1976, p. 224). The basic grant program was intended to provide all students with the minimum funding that they required to pursue an education beyond high school. The law not only ensured equal access to educational opportunity by expanding existing programs but also began to ensure student's equality of choice in educational opportunities (Gladieux and Wolanin, 1976). Two other provisions of the act served to stimulate equal opportunity. The first was the incorporation in the act of three existing equal opportunity programs: Upward Bound, Talent Search, and Special Services for the Disadvantaged. This incorporation was designed to ensure that a common effort was made to counsel minority and disadvantaged students to make use of higher education. The second was the inclusion of Title IX, which prohibited discrimination in educational activities on the basis of sex and thus removed numerous barriers to women in higher education.

Title IX has had far-reaching implications for the shape of higher education. Although it has been most frequently associated with intercollegiate athletics, its scope is much broader, including campus policy and regulations, student organizations, counseling, career placement services, housing, courses of study, and academic advising (Durrant, 1992; Gehring, 1993; Kadzielski, 1978). Title IX provided the basis for court rulings in the 1980s and 1990s dealing with issues of "sexual harassment by campus officials including faculty and staff (*Alexander v. Yale*, 1980; *Bougher v. University of Pittsburgh*, 1989)" (Gehring, 1993, p. 284). (The scope of Title IX has recently been expanded through the case of *Patricia H. v. Berkeley Unified School District* [1993], in which the court said that the "hostile environment" concept was applicable in the educational environment, under Title IX, as it was to the employment environment under Title VII. This holding has significant implications for the conduct of student services on campus.) A more detailed discussion of the impact of Title IX on campus administration is provided in Chapter Three of this work.

The principles of educational opportunity and access fostered by the Education Amendments of 1972 were supported by subsequent legislation. Section 504 of the Rehabilitation Act of 1973 prohibited discrimination on the basis of handicap. "The purpose of this act was to make higher education available to all qualified applicants regardless of physical disability" (Barr, 1989, p. 94). The Family Educational Rights and Privacy Act (FERPA) became law in 1974. FERPA, commonly known as the Buckley amendment, mandated institutional record keeping policies (Barr, 1989). FERPA tied compliance with the act's requirements to the receipt of Department of Education funding, either directly or through students receiving federal student aid. The act supported the new philosophy of student choice by giving students the right to inspect their institutional records, challenge the records if they believed they were inaccurate, and have recourse to a hearing if disputes arose. Finally, institutions were prohibited from releasing student records with certain exceptions without the written consent of the student (Barr, 1989).

A major revision of the definition of educational opportunity occurred in 1976 with the passage of the Middle Income Student Assistance Act (MISAA). MISAA represented the first major programmatic changes to the federal student aid programs since 1972. Although much of the attention during deliberation on the act focused on funding mechanisms (that is, increasing funding for the existing student aid programs or tuition tax credits), the primary outcome was an expansion of program eligibility to include students from middle-class families. The act was a policy and legislative response to the perception that middle-class students were being priced out of higher education while their parents were expected to bear an ever-increasing tax burden intended to support programs for which their children were not eligible. Numerous programmatic changes (for example, removing income caps from the Guaranteed Student Loan program) were implemented through MISAA, but it is its redefinition of financial need and broadening of eligibility that makes it important (Coomes, 1987).

In 1979, education in the United States earned cabinet-level status. "Unlike many other countries, for whom a centralized educational system was a vital component of nation-building, the United States traditionally avoided a strong federal role in education." ("Education Policy," 1981, p. 664). The first federal-level department of education had been created by Congress in 1867; however, it did not have cabinet-level status. Shortly after its creation, it was reclassified as a bureau in the Department of the Interior, and for its first seventy years focused on record keeping and information gathering on "modest federal education efforts" ("Education Policy," 1981, p. 664). The department was renamed the United States Office of Education in 1929 and became part of the Department of Health, Education, and Welfare in 1953. Candidate Jimmy Carter made the creation of a cabinet-level department of education a campaign promise, and in 1979, as president, he fulfilled his promise after having made the creation of such a program a primary legislative priority (Wilson, 1983). At the time of its creation, the Department of Education took responsibility for 150 education-related programs and became the fifth-largest department with the eighth-largest budget in the federal government ("Education Policy," 1981). The creation of the Department of Education represented a significant shift in federal policy toward education. Federal involvement that had begun with the Survey Ordinance of 1785 was formalized with the creation of the Department of Education—the federal government was firmly in the education business.

The 1980s: Paradoxical Demands

Like 1965, 1980 marked a watershed year in the higher education–federal government relationship. During that year, the Higher Education Act of 1965 was reauthorized with the passage of the Education Amendments of 1980. But, more importantly, 1980 was the year that the conservative Republican Ronald Reagan was elected president. The year marked the end of the liberal consensus that had guided higher education policy for the previous fifteen years, and it heralded a period of conflicting demands on postsecondary institutions and students (Finn, 1980).

The Education Amendments of 1980 were the last major piece of legislation enacted by the Carter administration and served as a bellwether for the subsequent actions that would be taken by the Reagan administration. The amendments were a hodgepodge of proposals that attempted to reconcile the Carter administration's goal of continuing program expansion that had reached its zenith in MISAA with an increasingly fiscally conservative Congress's calls to limit program growth. In an effort to meet the needs of the poorest students, Congress legislated an increase in the amount of Pell Grants for the neediest students. At the same time the legislation contained requirements intended to hold down costs, including increasing interest rates on student loans and creating a guaranteed but unsubsidized loan program for parents ("Education Policy," 1981). The Education Amendments of 1980 are not nearly as important as previous pieces of postsecondary legislation, but they illustrate the attempts to hold down costs that would be the hallmark of the new administration.

During the Reagan administration's tenure, the key characteristics of federal education policy were exhortative leadership, reduced funding, eliminated programs, devolution, and the de facto disestablishment of the federal education bureaucracy (Clark and Amiot, 1981; Clark and Astuto, 1986; Clark and Astuto, 1988; Doyle and Hartle, 1985). The new administration's higher education policy initiatives were part of a larger set of domestic policy concerns that included the "New Federalism," tax reform, and a reduction in the federal budget deficit. This agenda for education was shaped by a number of contextual issues that included President Reagan's previous experience with higher education as governor of California (Smith, 1980), a shift away from the education agenda of the "liberal consensus" (Finn, 1980), and the advent of fiscal conservatism in the nation's capital. That agenda consisted of a number of policy preferences that were intended to shape the procedural, as well as the substantive, direction of education into the 1990s. The procedural preferences established during the Reagan era included disestablishment (a reduced federal role in education), redirection (replacement of policy emphases in the federal role prominent in prior administrations), and devolution (the transfer of educational authority to state and local levels) (Clark and Astuto, 1986).

Among the substantive preferences, the most persistent message espoused by the Reagan administration and the one with the greatest impact on higher education was the call for reduced levels of federal support for education. The Reagan administration assumed office at the end of a period of unprecedented growth in education and in education funding. From 1965 to 1980, the contribution of the federal government to education grew in current dollars from $1.2 billion to $13.8 billion (Congressional Research Service, 1985). During that same time period, federal student aid funding increased from $45 million to $5.1 billion, an increase of 1,100 percent. To facilitate its general plans for economic recovery, the Reagan administration chose to reduce substantially federal support for social programs, including education. As a significant portion of the total education budget, student aid was targeted.

The 1982 budget process established the pattern for subsequent student aid budgets and provided the administration with its only major successes in diminishing federal financing for student aid. Savings were accomplished by modifying the Guaranteed Student Loan program and by beginning a four-year phase-out of the Social Security educational benefits program. The reduction of Social Security funds resulted in "750,000 students losing some benefits" (National Association of Student Financial Aid Administrators, 1988, p. 22). The early success the Reagan administration experienced with the 1982 budget established a pattern that carried forward through the budget for fiscal year 1988. That pattern was characterized by proposed funding reductions for all student aid programs, the elimination of programs that were perceived to be ineffectual, duplicative, or unnecessary, and the modification of eligibility standards to realize program savings.

While the Reagan administration was actively pushing for a more limited role for the federal government in higher education, members of Congress were passing legislation that resulted in increased intrusion in the lives of campuses and students. In 1982, Congress passed legislation linking receipt of federal financial aid to registration with the Selective Service Administration (Kaplin, 1985). Linking the federal aid application process to draft registration was actively opposed by members of the higher education community on the grounds that such a requirement would place an undue administrative burden on colleges and on the assumption that such a requirement was unconstitutional (National Association of Student Financial Aid Administrators, 1983, p. 2). Legal challenges to the new law were offered by colleges and civil liberties groups, but the "validity of . . . [the] requirement was upheld by the U.S. Supreme Court in *Selective Service System v. Minnesota Public Interest Research*, 104 S. Ct. 334 (1984)" (Kaplin, 1985, p. 276).

The Reagan administration was diligent in its calls for a reduction in funding for student aid and other programs supporting higher education. From 1981 through 1988, the administration proposed budgets for the federal student aid programs that were well below existing appropriation levels (Eaton, 1991). However, with the exception of the 1981 and 1982 fiscal years, Congress rejected the proposed massive cuts and funded student aid at existing or slightly increased appropriation levels throughout Ronald Reagan's tenure in office. Thus, during the 1980s, Congress was the primary protector of funding for postsecondary education. However, with the exception of fiscal 1985 (a budget approved during a general election year), Congress failed to appropriate sufficient funding for the Title IV student aid programs to allow them to keep pace with inflation (Eaton, 1991; Gillespie and Carlson, 1983; Gladieux, Knapp, and Merchant, 1992).

The Reagan administration's goal of substantially reducing federal investment was not realized. However, its unswerving calls for reduction retarded the growth of the programs and significantly shifted funding from grants to loans.

The 1990s: Reasserting a Federal Role?

If the 1970s were marked by an expansion of federal funding to ensure access and choice and the 1980s by efforts to restrain federal involvement in higher education, it appears that the 1990s will represent a period of increased federal intervention for the purpose of protecting students from a wide range of societal ills. The first of these new protective regulatory policies (Ripley and Franklin, 1986) was the Drug Free Schools and Communities Act Amendments passed on December 12, 1989. This legislation, targeted at schools, communities, and colleges, was an outgrowth of the federal "war on drugs" and was intended to reduce drug and alcohol use through increased education and information dissemination (Buchanan, 1993). Under this legislation, campuses are required to provide students and employees with a wide range of information on the legal and health risks of alcohol and drug possession and use. The Drug Free Schools and Communities Act Amendments were followed, in 1990, with the passage of the Student Right-to-Know and Campus Security Act. This legislation, like the Drug Free Schools and Communities Act Amendments, has as its fundamental purpose the protection of students through the provision of information. The Student Right-to-Know and Campus Security Act "requires colleges to collect data on certain crimes; to advise students, faculty, and staff in writing of such crimes; and to furnish information on police and other crime prevention services on an annual basis" (Buchanan, 1993, p. 502). As an apparent addendum to the main purpose of the bill and an excellent example of the use of legislation to address multiple and frequently unrelated issues, the Student Right-to-Know and Campus Security Act also contains provisions that require colleges to report statistics on the graduation rates of student athletes (Gehring, 1993). In 1992, the Campus Sexual Assault Victim's Bill of Rights was passed to address the concerns over increased sexual assaults on college campuses. This legislation requires that additional information be made available under the Student Right-to-Know and Campus Security Act. (A more in-depth discussion of the details of the Drug Free Schools and Communities Act Amendments, the Student Right-to-Know and Campus Security Act, and the Campus Sexual Assault Victim's Bill of Rights is provided by Gehring in Chapter Four.) Taken together, these three pieces of legislation attempt to address a wide range of campus problems through the provision of increased information to students and other campus constituents and represent an increased intervention on the part of the federal government in the day-to-day operation of college campuses.

Like 1981, 1993 marked the assumption in office of a new administration that was the complete antithesis of the administration that had preceded it. The Clinton administration's rhetoric seems to imply a return to many of the goals that drove federal higher education policy in the 1960s and 1970s. The early agenda of the Clinton administration included restructuring the federal student loan programs through the development of direct lending by institutions to students (a pilot direct-lending program was created by the Higher Education Act Amendments of 1992); the passage of the National and

Community Service Trust Act of 1993, which encourages participation in volunteer community service projects in return for vouchers good for payment of college tuition; and a continuation of the policies of fiscal restraint of the previous Republican administrations (Hartle, 1993). In assessing the early initiatives of the new administration, Hartle concludes that the Clinton administration will take a more activist position toward higher education, "but the mere fact of its activism does not necessarily mean it will always act in ways that please—or even benefit—the higher education community" (p. 18).

Outcomes of Federal Involvement

The role the federal government has played in shaping the interactions of campuses and students has grown significantly since passage of the Survey Ordinance of 1785. This section will offer a number of observations and conclusions based on the changing nature of that role.

Policy Ambiguity. For over two hundred years the federal government has used higher education as a solution to addressing diverse national policy problems. As a result there has never been, and still is not, a clear and comprehensive federal higher education policy. This lack of far-sighted higher education planning is attributable to the fact that, for most of the nation's history, higher education has not been a federal responsibility. Federal involvement in higher education has generally been an attempt to deal with noneducation-related problems, such as leadership training, public land development, a trained workforce, educational opportunity, a democratic citizenry, and international understanding (Gladieux and Wolanin, 1976). Gladieux and Wolanin emphasized the ambiguous nature of federal higher education policy:

> Another historical assumption of federal higher education policy is that there is *no* policy in the sense of an integrated and comprehensive blueprint. The federal government has had a profound influence on the development of higher education in the United States, but their influence has come about through a complex of federal activities lacking in central direction or vision.
>
> No coherent philosophical or administrative strategy characterizes the federal role in this area because higher education has been approached as a means to attain diverse federal policy ends [p. 7].

The lack of a coherent federal philosophy of higher education is a blessing and a curse. The main advantage is that individual programs (for example, Trio, Title IV student aid), once they have proven their value, are much more resistant to change because individual supporters continue to protect their own turf. Disadvantages include program duplication (for example, multiple student loan programs) and the use of colleges to address a wide range of only tangentially related social problems (for example, draft registration). With the multiple players currently involved in developing and directing federal higher education policy, it is doubtful whether any consensus on a clear and consistent philosophy can or will be developed.

The Development of Governmental-Educational Partnerships. As in many other policy arenas, higher education policy development has fostered the development and growth of a partnership between the forces of government and a wide range of higher education organizations and associations. These organizations include general higher education associations, like the American Council on Education; specific groups focused on the needs of a particular sector of higher education, like the American Association of Community Colleges; groups representing the interests and needs of higher education professionals, like the American College Personnel Association, state coordinating boards; and student and other grass-roots interest groups. This partnership frequently disagrees on specifics but is in general agreement on the value of higher education. As Hartmark and Hines (1986) state,

> In the governmental locus basic values are manifest in major policies, which are indications of public confidence in higher education or the public commitment to such goals as access and choice. This nation's longstanding leadership in science and technology, the nearly universal access it provides its citizens to higher education, and the significant public and private investment in higher education testify to the value this nation has historically placed on education. There is also another sense in which higher education is used as an instrument of social policy. Federal and state policies directed to affirmative action, accessibility for the disabled, health and safety regulations, federal training programs, etc., all exhibit this tendency by government to enlist the participation of higher education in activities deemed to advance public, governmentally sanctioned policy goals [p. 10].

Student Equity and Access. Achieving equal educational opportunity has been a goal of higher education since the passage of the Morrill Acts. That legislation was intended to expand the number and types of institutions so that more students would have the opportunity to secure a college education. The GI bills that followed World War II, the Korean War, and the Vietnam War expanded higher education by rewarding servicemen and women with financial benefits for their service. The expansion of higher education was supported by the 1947 Truman commission higher education report and realized through subsequent legislation, like the Higher Education Act of 1965, the Education Amendments of 1972, and the Middle Income Student Assistance Act of 1978. For nearly thirty years, federal student aid programs have been the primary vehicles utilized by the federal government for assuring equity and access. As Finn (1978) notes, "In American society, need-based student aid serves a dual purpose. It brings college within reach of people who might not otherwise be able—or willing—to enroll, and it also brings students to colleges that might not otherwise have enough students, at least not enough of the sort they favor" (p. 59). Numerous other federal initiatives, the Trio programs, Title IX of the Educational Amendments of 1972, Section 504 of the Rehabilitation Act of 1973, and the Americans with Disabilities Act, have all had significant impact on higher education by forcing colleges to modify their services and facilities to meet the needs of underrepresented student populations. Although higher education is still primarily a state responsibility, the federal government has increased its intervention most frequently through efforts to make college more accessible to all citizens.

The Role of Policy Entrepreneurs. "Policy innovation in higher education has largely been the product of policy entrepreneurs in the executive branch and Congress . . . . Policy entrepreneurship refers to a situation in which elite political actors are able to formulate and advance new policies largely on their own initiative. It assumes that broad popular, partisan or group support can make higher education an attractive but not compelling arena for policy innovation. Entrepreneurs are left sufficient flexibility to choose among arenas of activity, to define the character of their involvement and the substance of their initiative, and to mobilize support for their decisions" (Conlan, 1981, p. 51).

From Justin Morrill to William Jefferson Clinton, policy entrepreneurs have shaped the federal government's role in higher education. The venue of the policy entrepreneur has varied. At times, it has centered in the executive branch. President Lyndon Johnson, the teacher in the White House, pushed for equity programs that emerged as College Work Study, Educational Opportunity Grants, and Guaranteed Student Loans. With his gubernatorial record of involvement in education and a strong preference for domestic policy making, President Clinton appears to be a much more active education president than either of his two immediate predecessors (Hartle, 1993). Although health care and welfare reform have been the primary focus of the first eighteen months of the Clinton administration, it is not unreasonable to assume that other initiatives to shape and influence higher education will be forthcoming.

With the exception of President Clinton, the majority of policy entrepreneurs who have shaped federal higher education policy since the Johnson administration have been members of Congress. Congresswoman Edith Green and Senator Claiborne Pell shaped the discussion of expanding federal student aid in the 1970s. Senator Pell's role in that process was recognized when Congress renamed the BEOG program the Pell Grant program in 1980.

Programmatic Growth. Since 1958, the involvement of the federal government in higher education has expanded exponentially. In 1958, the year that the National Defense Education Act was passed, federal funds for higher education totaled $1.06 billion. The NDEA contained ten titles, covering seven programs ("Federal Education Programs . . . ," 1965). By comparison, federal on-budget funds for postsecondary education for fiscal year 1993 totaled $17.03 billion, an increase of 1,500 percent (Snyder and Hoffman, 1993). The Higher Education Amendments of 1992 contained fifteen titles covering more than thirty programs ranging from Pell Grants and Federal Robert T. Stafford Student Loans to the Trio programs, the Fund for the Improvement of Higher Education (FIPSE), and a newly created Direct Loan Program demonstration project ("Higher Education Act Provisions," 1992). Clearly, the federal government is no longer just an ancillary player in the higher education arena.

Restrictive Legislation and Legal Decisions. This section began with the assertion that the federal government has greatly expanded its role in the postsecondary arena. But expanded programmatic offerings, enhanced student equity, access, and choice, and increased financial support come at a cost. That cost has been restrictive legislation and legal decisions that have led to decreased campus autonomy. Campuses must now respond to a variety of federal mandates, ranging from reporting campus crime statistics to making physical facilities more accessible to the disabled. Whether campus administrators believe that the benefits of federal programs outweigh the increased level of federal intervention remains to be seen. One perspective on this new trend toward increased federal intervention will be offered by Gehring in Chapter Six.

Conclusion

Federal involvement in higher education has resulted in a number of positive outcomes for campuses and students. More people attend college in the United States than in any other nation. This expansion of opportunity (Brubacher and Rudy, 1976) has been an important result of federal intervention. A major challenge facing the United States in the next century will be economic competitiveness. As many have noted, at the heart of economic competitiveness is a well-educated workforce. Colleges will play an integral role in the continuing development of that workforce as well as in other important national programs, like basic research. The federal government has a stake in seeing that the goals of economic and human capital development are realized (Hartle, 1993). Those goals can only be realized through continued federal involvement in the higher education arena; that involvement will have a continued impact on the lives of students.

References

Barr, M. J. "Legal Issues Confronting Student Affairs Practice." In U. Delworth, G. Hanson, and Associates, *Student Services: A Handbook for the Profession.* (2nd ed.) San Francisco: Jossey-Bass, 1989.

Brubacher, J. S., and Rudy, W. *Higher Education in Transition: A History of American Colleges and Universities.* New York: HarperCollins, 1976.

Buchanan, E. T. "The Changing Role of Government in Higher Education." In M. J. Barr and Associates, *The Handbook of Student Affairs Administration.* San Francisco: Jossey-Bass, 1993.

Caro, R. A. *The Path to Power: The Years of Lyndon Johnson.* New York: Knopf, 1982.

Clark, D. L., and Amiot, M. A. "The Impact of the Reagan Administration on Federal Education Policy." *The Phi Delta Kappan,* 1981, *63,* 258–262.

Clark, D. L., and Astuto, T. A. *The Significance and Permanence of Changes in Federal Education Policy: 1980–1988.* Bloomington, Ind.: Policy Studies Center of the University Council for Educational Administration, 1986.

Clark, D. L., and Astuto, T. A. *Education Policy After Reagan— What Next?* Charlottesville, Va.: Policy Studies Center of the University Council for Educational Administration, 1988.

Clinton, W. J. "Remarks on Signing the National and Community Service Trust Act of 1993." *Weekly Compilation of Presidential Documents,* Sept. 27, 1993, pp. 1822–1824.

Commager, H. S. (ed.). *Documents of American History.* (6th ed.) New York: Appleton-Century-Crofts, 1958.

Congressional Research Service. *Reauthorization of the Higher Education Act: Program Descriptions, Issues, and Options.* Washington, D.C.: United States Government Printing Office, 1985.

Conlan, T. J. *The Federal Role in the Federal System: The Dynamics of Growth.* Vol. 6. *The Evolution of a Problematic Partnership: The Feds and Higher Education.* Washington, D.C.: Advisory Commission on Intergovernmental Relations, 1981.

Coomes, M. D. *An Examination of Changes in Federal Student Financial Aid Policy from 1981 to 1985–1986.* Unpublished doctoral dissertation, Indiana University, Bloomington, 1987.

Cultice, W. W. *Youth's Battle for the Ballot: A History of Voting Age in America.* New York: Greenwood Press, 1992.

Davis, J. R. "The Higher Education Act of 1972: A New Form of Aid to Private Colleges and Universities." *Intellect,* 1972, *101,* 157–159.

Doyle, D. P., and Hartle, D. H. "Ideology, Pragmatic Politics, and the Education Budget." In J. C. Weicher (ed.), *Maintaining the Safety Net: Income Redistribution Programs in the Reagan Administration.* Washington, D.C.: American Enterprise Institute for Public Policy Research, 1985.

Durrant, S. M. "Title IX—Its Power and Its Limitation." *The Journal of Physical Education, Recreation and Dance,* 1992, *63*(3), 60–64.

Eaton, J. S. *The Unfinished Agenda: Higher Education and the 1980s.* New York: Macmillan, 1991.

"Education Policy." *Congress and the Nation: A Review of Government and Politics.* Vol. 5, 1977–1980. Washington, D.C.: Congressional Quarterly Service, 1981.

"Federal Education Programs: Federal Aid to Education." *Congress and the Nation: A Review of Government and Politics in the Post-War Years.* Vol. 1, 1945–1964. Washington, D.C.: Congressional Quarterly Service, 1965.

"Federal Education Programs." *Congress and the Nation: A Review of Government and Politics.* Vol. 2, 1965–1968. Washington, D.C.: Congressional Quarterly Service, 1969.

"Federal Education Programs." *Congress and the Nation: A Review of Government and Politics.* Vol. 3, 1969–1972. Washington, D.C.: Congressional Quarterly Service, 1973.

Fenske, R. H. "Student Aid Past and Present." In R. H. Fenske, R. P. Huff, and Associates, *Handbook of Student Financial Aid.* San Francisco: Jossey-Bass, 1983.

Fenske, R. H. "Historical Foundations of Student Services." In U. Delworth, G. Hanson, and Associates, *Student Services: A Handbook for the Profession.* (2nd ed.) San Francisco: Jossey-Bass, 1989a.

Fenske, R. H. "Evolution of the Student Services Profession." In U. Delworth, G. Hanson, and Associates, *Student Services: A Handbook for the Profession.* (2nd ed.) San Francisco: Jossey-Bass, 1989b.

Finn, C. E., Jr. *Scholars, Dollars, and Bureaucrats.* Washington, D.C.: Brookings Institute, 1978.

Finn, C. E., Jr. "The Future of Education's Liberal Consensus." *Change,* 1980, *12*(6), 25–30.

Fleming, J. *The Lengthening Shadow of Slavery: A Historical Justification for Affirmative Action for Blacks in Higher Education.* Washington, D.C.: Howard University Press, 1976.

Gehring, D. D. "Understanding Legal Constraints on Practice." In M. J. Barr and Associates, *The Handbook of Student Affairs Administration.* San Francisco: Jossey-Bass, 1993.

Gillespie, D. A., and Carlson, N. *Trends in Student Aid: 1963–1983.* Washington, D.C.: College Entrance Examination Board, 1983.

Gladieux, L. E. "Future Direction for Student Aid." In R. H. Fenske, R. P. Huff, and Associates, *Handbook of Student Financial Aid.* San Francisco: Jossey-Bass, 1983.

Gladieux, L. E., Knapp, L. G., and Merchant, R. *Trends in Student Aid: 1982–1992.* Washington, D.C.: College Entrance Examination Board, 1992.

Gladieux, L. E., and Wolanin, T. R. *Congress and the Colleges*. Lexington, Mass.: Lexington Books, 1976.

Hartle, T. W. "The Clinton Administration Takes Charge: What Next for Higher Education?" *Educational Record*, 1993, *74*(4), 14–19.

Hartmark, L. S., and Hines, E. R. "Politics and Policy in Higher Education: Reflections on the Status of the Field." In S. K. Gove and T. M. Stauffer (eds.), *Policy Controversies in Higher Education* (pp. 3–26). New York: Greenwood Press, 1986.

"Higher Education Act Provisions." *1992 Congressional Quarterly Almanac*. Washington, D.C.: Congressional Quarterly, 1992.

Higher Education for American Democracy: A Report of the President's Commission on Higher Education. Washington, D.C.: U.S. Government Printing Office, 1947.

Kadzielski, M. A. "Title IX and Residential Living: An Analysis." *NASPA Journal*, 1978, *16*(1), 29–32.

Kaplin, W. H. *The Law of Higher Education: A Comprehensive Guide to Legal Implications of Administrative Decision Making*. (2nd ed.) San Francisco: Jossey-Bass, 1985.

King, L. *The Washington Lobbyists for Higher Education*. Lexington, Mass.: Lexington Books, 1975.

Kluger, R. *Simple Justice: The History of Brown v. Board of Education and Black America's Struggle for Equality*. New York: Knopf, 1976.

Moore, J. W. "Purposes and Provisions of Federal Programs." In R. H. Fenske, R. P. Huff, and Associates, *Handbook of Student Financial Aid*. San Francisco: Jossey-Bass, 1983.

National Association of State Universities and Land Grant Colleges. *In Brief: Facts About U.S. Higher Education, Public Higher Education and NASULGC Institutions*. Washington, D.C.: National Association of State Universities and Land Grant Colleges, 1994.

National Association of Student Financial Aid Administrators. *Selective Service Registration and Student Aid: A Chronological Review of Events*. Washington, D.C.: National Association of Student Financial Aid Administrators, 1983.

National Association of Student Financial Aid Administrators. *Student Aid During the Reagan Administration: An Analysis of the FY-89 Proposals and an Historical Review* (NASFAA Special Report No. 24). Washington, D.C.: National Association of Student Financial Aid Administrators, 1988.

"1972 Education Act: $21 Billion in Aid, Bussing Curbs." *1972 Congressional Quarterly Almanac*. Washington, D.C.: Congressional Quarterly, 1972.

Rainsford, G. N. *Congress and Higher Education in the Nineteenth Century*. Knoxville: University of Tennessee Press, 1972.

Ripley, R. B., and Franklin, G. A. *Policy Implementation and Bureaucracy*. (2nd ed.) Chicago: Dorsey Press, 1986.

Rivlin, A. *The Role of the Federal Government in Financing Higher Education*. Washington, D.C.: Brookings Institute, 1961.

Rudolph, F. *The American College and University: A History*. Athens: University of Georgia Press, 1990.

Smith, M. "Lessons from the California Experience." *Change*, 1980, *12*(6), 32–39.

Snyder, T. D., and Hoffman, C. M. *Digest of Education Statistics: 1993*. Washington, D.C.: National Center for Education Statistics, 1993.

"The Unique Role and Mission of Historically Black Colleges and Universities: Hearing before the Subcommittee on Postsecondary Education of the Committee on Education and Labor." House of Representatives, 100th Congress, Second Session. Hearing held in Durham, N.C., Sept. 12, 1988 (Serial No. 100–98). Washington, D.C.: U.S. Government Printing Office, 1988.

Wilson, J. T. *Academic Science, Higher Education, and the Federal Government, 1950–1983*. Chicago: University of Chicago Press, 1983.

Cases

Alexander v. Yale, 631 F. 2d 178 (2nd Cir. 1980).
Bougher v. University of Pittsburgh, 882 F.2d 74 (3rd Cir. 1989).
Brown v. Board of Education, 347 U.S. 483 (1954).
Dixon v. Alabama State Board of Education, 294 F. 2d 150 (5th Cir. 1961).
Florida ex rel. Hawkins v. Board of Control, 350 U.S. 413 (1956).
Gott v. Berea College, 161 S. W. 204 (Ky. 1913).
Healy v. James, 408 U.S. 169 (1972).
Patricia H. v. Berkeley Unified School District, 830 F.Supp. 1288 (N.D. Cal. 1993).
Plessy v. Ferguson, 163 U.S. 537 (1896).
Selective Service System v. Minnesota Public Interest Research, 104 S. Ct. 334 (1984).
Tinker v. Des Moines, 393 U.S. 503 (1969).

MICHAEL D. COOMES is assistant professor of higher education and student affairs at Bowling Green State University.

*This chapter presents definitions of policy, explains the policy process,
and offers suggestions on how campus administrators can shape the
development of educational policy.*

The Policy Process

Michael D. Coomes, Donald Hossler

The assistant director of financial aid establishing a student's eligibility for a
Stafford Loan, the director of campus safety and security filing an institution's
annual crime statistics, and the director of judicial affairs overseeing a hearing
of the university's judicial board are all fulfilling responsibilities mandated or
influenced by federal policies and procedures. These administrators, as well as
many others, are required to interpret, implement, and react to federal legislation, regulations, and legal opinions that they may only vaguely understand
and had little or no hand in developing. To assist those professionals in understanding the process that leads to the policies they are required to implement,
this chapter will define the term policy and examine its relationship to politics; explain the purposes of a number of different generic types of policies;
describe the policy process; discuss different policy formulation mechanisms
(for example, Congress, the judiciary); and suggest ways that campus administrators can influence the policy process.

Policy and Politics: A Symbiotic Relationship

Bhola (1975) defines policy making as "a political process concerned with new
social outcomes, it should always be envisioning new uses of power to create
new or qualitatively new power relationships or distributions of goods in con-
gruence with the newly established set of power relationships, that is, alternative social hierarchies. Conversely, if there is no intent toward creating a new
pattern of power relationships or obtaining a new distribution of economic,
educational or social goods, then it is *not* [author's emphasis] policy we are
concerned with; we may be concerned merely with rules and regulations"
(p. 8). Similarly, Hartmark and Hines (1986) define policy as "purposive

collective action directed toward the solution of a societal problem or the resolution of a common issue. Policy does not happen; it is 'made' through a complex, more or less, deliberative process, which can be characterized as having various stages" (p. 6).

Politics and policy are frequently viewed as a single process, but although there is a natural relationship between the two, they are not the same. Whereas policy focuses on the *what* of the process, politics encompasses the *how* and the *whom* (Hartmark and Hines, 1986). Policy should be "viewed in terms of the content or substantive purpose of decision making" (Hartmark and Hines, 1986, p. 7). It is a series of actions designed to bring about a specific outcome or set of outcomes. Politics involves how that process plays itself out, the various influences that are brought to bear at leverage points within the policy process (Gergen, 1968), and the people and organizations who attempt to influence the process. The primary emphasis of this chapter will be on defining the policy process, that is, the set of actions that start with an idea designed to redistribute goods or services and ends with programs that carry out that idea. We will conclude the chapter with a discussion of the various leverage points where politics intersect with the policy process. It is through these leverage points that student affairs practitioners have the opportunity to shape the outcomes of the policy process.

Policy Types

Scholars working in the field of policy studies have advanced several classifications for the various types of policies. It is beyond the scope of this chapter to explore fully the types of policies. Bull (n.d.) suggests that there are sixteen different types of policies, seventeen different ways in which a policy may designate the occasion for action, and sixteen ways to designate the agent responsible for acting on a policy. A three-dimensional matrix using these classificatory variables results in 4,352 types of policies! No attempt will be made to explain all of them, but some useful exemplars of policy frameworks have been selected. Wirt and Kirst (1989) identify five types of policy values or goals that are common in educational legislation. These include the following four goals:

1. Choice: The goal of choice is exemplified by legislated options that ensure choices for constituent groups. (Some financial aid observers, for example, have suggested that one of the historic purposes of student financial aid was not only to provide access to higher education but also to provide students choices between a range of institutions.)
2. Efficiency: The goal of efficiency is exemplified by economic assumptions that seek to maximize gains and minimize costs or accountability assumptions that seek to provide mechanisms of oversight for superiors. (The 1992 Higher Education Act, which includes legislation that attempts to reduce default rates through the provision of funds to state postsecondary

education agencies for the creation of State Postsecondary Review Entities [SPRE] is an example of the efficiency approach.)

3. Equity: The goal of equity is exemplified by equalizing or redistributing public resources to meet morally desirable ends. (This is certainly one of the principal reasons for the creation of federal and state financial aid programs.)

4. Quality: The goal of quality is exemplified by the use of public resources to achieve or require professionally determined standards of excellence and proficiency. (Once again, we might point to the federal mandate to create SPREs or the inclusion of student measures of progress toward degree completion in federal aid legislation as examples of attempts by policy makers to legislate quality among postsecondary educational institutions.)

Another example of classification systems developed for public policies is found in the work of Odden (1991). Odden notes that in social programs, like in education, there are two types of federal policies—developmental and redistributive. Developmental policies are those in which most local or state governments are already involved. Because of the already established interests and local or state governmental efforts, federal policies tend to support and reinforce these efforts. As a result, federal policies are implemented quickly with "a relatively uncontentious implementation process" (p. 7). Changes in federal financial aid policies during the late 1970s and the 1980s, after most states had also become heavily involved in providing student aid, might be viewed as developmental policies.

Redistributive policies, in contrast, tend to force local or state governments into programs and activities in which they had not been previously involved. Implementation of redistributive programs is contentious. These policies are usually eventually implemented but not without a series of rules and regulations that require a prolonged process of adaptation at the local or state level. The current effort of the federal government to force states to become more involved in the accreditation of postsecondary educational institutions through the creation of SPREs is an example of a redistributive policy that is drawing criticism from states and private accrediting bodies.

The Policy Process

Policy making is frequently envisioned as two distinct processes: (1) policy formulation and legitimation; and (2) policy implementation (Ripley and Franklin, 1986). Although this may be an overly simplistic description, it is useful in helping one understand that what many see as policy making—the interaction of politics and governance that results in legislation, administrative rule making, and legal opinion—is just the first step in a longer process. As Lipsky (1980) notes, legislators may make policy, but it is the actions of street-level bureaucrats that make policy real. In Chapter Five, Schuh and Ogle discuss the role of student affairs administrators (or collegiate street-level bureaucrats) in interpreting and implementing policy at the campus level.

Table 2.1. The Policy Process

System	Activities	Output
	Problem-to-Government Phase	
Problem identification	Perception (receiving and registering an event)	Problem
	Definition (bringing into sharp relief the effect of an event)	
	Aggregation (grouping)	
	Organization (developing structure)	
	Representation (developing and maintaining access)	Demand
	Agenda setting (theories, strategies)	Agendas 1. Problem definition 2. Proposal 3. Bargaining 4. Continuing
	Action-in-Government Phase	
Program development	Formulation (developing a plan, a method, a prescription for acting on a problem): Includes routine, analogous, and creative formulation.	Proposal
Legitimacy (authorizing and supporting government)	Legitimation (approving a proposal by an accepted means—importance of majority coalition building)	Program
	Appropriation (approving program funds) 1. Formulation 2. Legitimation	Budget
	Government-to-Problem Phase	
Program implementation	Organization (establishing administrative methods and units)	Structure
	Interpretation (translating authorization into acceptable feasible directives—importance of discretion)	Working rules/standards
	Application (routine provision of services, payments, controls—importance of "mutual role taking")	Varies (depends on program)
	Program-to-Government Phase	
Program evaluation	Evaluation (judging the merit of programs—as functional activity in all systems; as a systematic endeavor for specific programs) 1. Specification (setting purposes, criteria) 2. Measurement (collecting data—systematic, unsystematic) 3. Analysis (reviewing data—systematic, unsystematic) 4. Recommendation (proposing change)	Varies (depends on findings)

(Emergence of policy cycles of support, incremental adjustment, program change, redefinition or discovery of problems)

System	Activities	Output
	Problem Resolution or Change Phase	
Program termination	Resolution (effecting change in public problems)	Relative solution; social change
	Termination	

Source: Jones, 1977. ©Wadsworth Publishing Co. Reprinted by permission.

The full policy-making process has been outlined by numerous authors (Brewer and DeLeon, 1983; Gilbert, 1984; Kelman, 1987; Lindbloom, 1968; Ripley and Franklin, 1986). All of these formulations bear a striking resemblance to one another. Common phases or steps in the process include identification of the problem, generation of alternative solutions, selection of an appropriate solution, implementation of the solution, and, finally, evaluation of the solution. For the purpose of this discussion, the model formulated by Jones (1977) and Jones and Matthes (1983) will be described in greater detail. Table 2.1 outlines Jones's original model of the policy process.

The Jones model is characterized by four major concepts; *phases, systems, functional activities,* and *outputs.* Each of these necessitates a brief discussion. *Phases* (such as the problem to government phase) focus on the central concern of policy making, that is "what government does to act on public problems" (Jones, 1977, p. 10). *Systems* "refer to two or more persons engaged in patterned or structured interaction guided by shared values and directed toward the achievement of some goal" (Jones, 1977, p. 11). Jones notes the following systems inherent in the policy process: (1) problem identification; (2) formulation; (3) legitimation; (4) implementation; and (5) evaluation. In turn, each of these systems is characterized by a set of *functional activities* or processes, inputs that must be responded to or actions that need to be taken to resolve the major task of the system. These functional activities will be described in greater detail shortly. Finally, *outputs* are the outcomes of governmental interaction in the policy process. In the early phases of the model, outputs consist of identified and defined problems. In the latter phases the outputs become programs or budgets.

To summarize, Jones views the policy process as a sequence of phases outlining the government's response to public problems. These phases address a central concern—what Jones terms systems—for example, problem identification. In turn, these concerns consist of a set of functional activities, the resolution of which results in an output or outcome. This formulation of the policy process is particularly useful for three reasons: (1) it notes the relationship of governmental action to environmental conditions (the phases of the model); (2) it outlines a detailed sequence of activities that constitute the policy-making process; and (3) it identifies the various products (such as problems, proposals, programs) of the policy process. Focusing on government/environment interaction, formal processes, and products and outcomes presents a more complete and complex picture of the process that results in policies that affect colleges. The following sections will examine the phases of the policy process in greater detail.

Problem-to-Government Phase. The central concern in the problem-to-government phase is problem identification. Campus crime is not a new phenomenon. Rudolph (1990) notes the prevalence of assault, verbal abuse, property damage, and drunkenness in early American colleges. However, it was not until 1991 that Congress felt compelled to address the issue by amending the Higher Education Act of 1965 to include the Student Right-to-

Know and Campus Security Act. For whatever reasons, by the 1980s campus crime was perceived as a public problem that necessitated a policy response. Thus, the first steps in the policy process are the perception and definition of an issue or event as a public problem. Problems reach the policy agenda through a wide range of activities including internal and external catastrophic events like earthquakes and war (Cobb and Elder, 1972); political promises made during election campaigns (Jones, 1977); and the efforts of motivated individuals or groups who either have been confronted with the problem or have an ideological perspective that necessitates raising a particular issue to public problem status.

Once problems are identified, the arduous task of problem definition begins. The problem definition step is perspectival (Schwartz and Ogilvy, 1979; Kuh, Whitt, and Shedd, 1987). Different assumptions about the nature of the problem will lead to different alternative solutions to it. For example, perceiving that assaults against women on campus are being carried out by strangers, will engender a different response from policy makers than if those assaults are perceived to be carried out by acquaintances.

Once a problem has been perceived and defined, the focus turns to the functional activities of aggregation/organization, representation, and agenda setting (Jones, 1977). Although some problems are brought to government by individuals, most are brought to governmental attention by aggregates of people working in an organized fashion. As Jones (1977) notes, "The number of people affected, the extent to which they aggregate, and the degree and type of organization all may influence the policy process and the particular outcome in regard to the problems being acted on" (p. 28).

The most common way for organized aggregates to raise and support positions on problems is through the election of policy makers to positions in government and through the development of representational lobbies. Postsecondary education has spawned numerous associations (examples include the Association of American Universities; the American Association of Community and Junior Colleges; the American Association of State Colleges and Universities; the National Association of Independent Colleges and Universities; the National Association of College and University Business Officers; the National Association of State Universities and Land Grant Colleges; the National Association of Student Personnel Associations; the United States Student Association) which have as their purpose the representation of various constituents to policy makers in government (Bloland, 1985; Hawkins, 1992). These associations assist in the process that links people, problems, and government (Jones, 1977).

The activities of problem identification and definition, aggregation/ organization, and representation lead to agenda setting (Anderson, 1975; Cobb and Elder, 1972; Wise, 1991). Agendas may be systemic, that is, encompassing all the problems facing a political community that are the legitimate purview of government (Cobb and Elder, 1972; Jones, 1977). Examples of systemic agenda items include national defense and public welfare. Agendas may also be more discrete, constituting governmental or institutional agendas (Anderson, 1975; Cobb and Elder, 1972; Jones, 1977). Such agendas focus on the more immediate issues that government decision makers face at a particular point in time. During recent congressional deliberations, the institutional agenda included discussions of health care reform and crime control.

Problems may be new or newly perceived as public problems necessitating a policy response. As Jones (1977) noted, "Most of what government acts on results from the continuing application and evaluation of ongoing programs" (p. 10). Excellent examples are the federal financial aid programs. Legislation requires that the student aid programs be reauthorized every five years. Although the process occasionally results in new programmatic interventions, the more frequent result is that existing programs are modified to meet changing institutional and student needs and budgetary constraints. Even then, those changes are incremental, not revolutionary in nature (Gladieux and Wolanin, 1976; Lindbloom, 1959, 1979). As the title of an article in the *Chronicle of Higher Education* published shortly before passage of the Higher Education Act of 1992 put it, "College Officials Say Politics and Budgetary Constraints Have Doomed Reauthorization Bill's Promise of Reform" (DeLoughry, 1992).

Action-in-Government Phase. When problems reach institutional agendas, the primary task for government becomes program development. Program development requires policy makers to formulate policy proposals, legitimize programs, and appropriate funds (Jones, 1977).

Formulation is the first process in the action-in-government phase and a refinement of the problem identification/description process. The formulation task, called *estimation* by Brewer and DeLeon (1983), involves the "systematic investigation of a problem and a thoughtful assessment of options and alternatives" (p. 83). Formulation then involves the generation of plans to address identified problems. Jones (1977) notes that a number of conditions shape the formulation of policy proposals. Those conditions include: (a) more than one set of actors supporting competing or similar proposals, (b) clearly defined or ill-constructed problems, and (c) the fact that formulation may take place "over a long period of time without ever building sufficient support for any one proposal" (p. 50). In addition, during the formulation process, supporters of alternative proposals have the opportunity to seek support for those proposals at a number of "appeal points." Finally, Jones points out, the formulation "process itself is never neutral" (Jones, 1977, p. 50).

The evolution of federal student financial aid policy may serve as a useful example for understanding many of the analytical perspectives of policy research. In the early 1970s, rising educational costs coupled with a desire to increase access to postsecondary education made expanding the federal government's student aid program an important issue for Congress. Two plans for addressing the financial needs of students were formulated. One plan, supported by Congresswoman Edith Green (D-OR), called for providing increased aid to institutions, both in the form of additional aid for the existing student aid programs (for example, the Educational Opportunity Grant program) and in the form of direct aid to institutions. A second proposal, proffered by Senator Claiborne Pell (D-RI) and supported by the Nixon White House, called for the creation of an entitlement program of direct aid to students. After much debate, political wrangling, and modification, the second formulation was adopted with passage of the Education Amendments of 1972 and the creation of the Basic Educational Opportunity Grant (now the Pell Grant) program (Gladieux and Wolanin, 1976).

As this example illustrates, problems do and should generate many possible solutions. Deciding on a single intervention from a range of alternatives involves the process of legitimation. Program legitimation, which is primarily a function of the legislative branch, is "the process of getting the approval of those who count.... In general, ... one can say that those persons count who have the authority to say *yes* or *no* and who have the interest, organization, and resources to be heard on the subject. Getting approval, then, typically requires getting support from those with authority and interest" (Jones, 1977, p. 133). In representative governments like ours, getting approval from those who can say yes requires majority coalition building (Jones, 1977), access to decision makers, political skills, and perseverance. Majority coalition building through legislative processes may be the primary means of building legitimation. However, other means of establishing legitimation exist, including hierarchical authority, professionalism, efficiency, and citizen participation (Jones and Matthes, 1983). Of special note for postsecondary education is the role of professionalism. As public policy problems become increasingly complex, the role of the professional in analyzing the scope and importance of a problem and in suggesting alternative solutions also becomes more critical. During the 1992 reauthorization of the Higher Education Act, Congress turned to experts—for example, financial aid officers, needs analysis processors like the College Scholarship Service, and professional associations like the National Association of Financial Aid Administrators—to provide guidance on how to improve the highly complex and very confusing student aid delivery system (Rothschild, 1992). As experts on students and university operations, student affairs educators should view themselves as professionals who can lend their expertise to legitimate various government programs, thus establishing a potentially important new role for student affairs practitioners in the policy process.

The final activity in the problem in government phase is appropriating funds. The governmental budgeting process has become so complex and so constrained by laws like the Credit Reform Act and the 1991 Budget Agreement that it has become its own method of shaping and directing public policy. No longer are federal education programs reevaluated and modified only during the reauthorization process, every five years. Now they are under constant evaluation and modification, through the annual appropriations process. For example, the authorizing legislation for the Pell Grants, a quasi entitlement program, guarantees a specific level of funding for eligible students. However, appropriations for Pell Grants have been historically underfunded, resulting in the necessity to make modifications to Pell Grant funding formulas in appropriation bills. These changes have caused much consternation on the part of student aid officers, who have had to modify their awarding procedures to adapt to changing funding levels. Some government mandates, like those contained in the Drug Free Schools and Communities Act Amendments of 1989, are not funded by government and place the burden of funding on the affected institutions. This raises the question of whether programs without funding can be considered programs at all.

Government-to-Problem Phase. Legislation creates programs, and programs must be implemented. As noted earlier, implementation is frequently conceptualized as separate from the policy formulation process. Implementation has gotten considerable attention as policy analysts realize that the implementation process has a life of its own that frequently results in numerous unintended outcomes (Lipsky, 1980; Pressman and Wildavsky, 1973; Ripley and Franklin, 1986).

Implementation is defined as follows, "Those activities directed toward putting a program into effect. Three sets of activities are significant: interpretation—the translation of program language into acceptable and feasible directives; organization—the establishment of units and methods for putting a program into effect; and application—the routine provision of services, payments, or other agreed-upon program objectives or instruments" (Jones, 1977, p. 139).

Although Congress will frequently note intent in final legislative language, the interpretation of legislation usually is left to the administrative agency with oversight responsibility for the area that the law addresses. Interpretation is frequently accomplished through the regulatory process. This process begins with the enactment of legislation and proceeds to an analysis of the legislation, including an analysis of the intent of Congress in passing the legislation. For higher education legislation, the analysis and review stage of the process includes analyzing the legislation to determine if regulations are warranted, preparing and reviewing draft regulations from appropriate staff in the Department of Education, securing approval of regulations from the secretary of education, and if approved by the secretary, securing approval of draft legislation from the Office of Management and Budget (OMB) (General Accounting Office, 1990). Once draft legislation is approved it is published as a proposed regulation in the Federal Register for public comment. Section 431 of the General Education Provisions Act prohibits proposed regulations from taking effect sooner than thirty days after their publication. Frequently the period for public comment is longer than thirty days. Public comments are received by the designated agency and analyzed, and, when deemed appropriate, changes are incorporated in the regulations. Revised final regulations follow the incorporation of public comments, the review regulations by agency heads, and if needed, agency responses to letters from member of Congress (General Accounting Office, 1990, p. 3). The process ends with the publication of final regulations in the *Federal Register.*

From start to finish, the process is long and involved to ensure that the public, particularly relevant stakeholder groups, are given ample opportunity for comment and influence. This desire to consider how the law should be implemented frequently results in considerable delay between the passage of legislation and the promulgation of final regulations. The entire process is required to take no longer than 240 days, but a General Accounting Office (GAO) report (1990) of eighty-three sets of regulations reviewed by DOE and OMB disclosed that only thirteen met the 240-day standard. The average issuance time for eighty of the eighty-three regulations (three had not been issued at the time of the GAO report) was 389 days, with a range of 63 to 912 days. Obviously, a wait of nearly three years for final regulations presents considerable problems for campus administrators looking for guidance in setting up programmatic interventions.

Implementation, like the policy formulation process, is chaotic, open to interpretation, and frequently idiosyncratic. Ripley and Franklin (1986) note the limitations on effective implementation: "Implementation processes involve *many important actors* holding *diffuse and competing goals* and *expectations* who work within a *context of an increasingly large and complex mix of government programs* that require *participation from numerous layers and units of government* and who are affected by *powerful factors beyond their control* [authors' emphasis]" (p. 11).

Administrators who have been required to interpret federal intent and implement federal programs on their campuses are undoubtedly aware of the difficulties implementation presents. Advice on how campus administrators can effectively implement federal mandates and programs is discussed further by Schuh and Ogle in Chapter Five.

Program-to-Government Phase. Like all good models of decision-making and professional practice (Strange and King, 1990), the feedback loop of evaluation is essential to effective program operation. Some type of evaluation is necessary for governmental policy makers to determine if programmatic services and requirements are meeting intended program goals. Program evaluation can be formative or summative. It can be carried out by internal program administrators or external evaluators, employ quantitative or qualitative methods (or a combination of the two), focus on the substance of policy or on the policy process, and have a large scale or focus on a single program of services at a single site. Like implementation, the need to conduct effective and efficient evaluations of policy has resulted in an entire literature on policy analysis. Examples of this literature include the work of Brewer and DeLeon (1983); Cronbach and others (1980); Hartmark and Hines (1986); Madaus, Scrivin, and Stufflebeam (1988); Nachmias (1979); Paris and Reynolds (1983); and White (1983).

The literature on policy evaluation is full of descriptions of the difficulties associated with evaluating the impact of social programs (Hearn, 1993). Evaluation, like the other parts of the policy process, includes a set of processes and procedures as well as a wide range of value-laden issues. These issues include the following: What should be evaluated? When should evaluations be conducted? Who should conduct evaluations and with what methods? How should evaluation results be utilized? Determining such things as appropriate measures of the outcomes of a policy, the possibility of unintended outcomes, the effects of funding, and the changing goals of those who commission evaluation studies are some of the difficulties in conducting policy evaluations. All of these questions, as well as others, need to be considered if evaluation is to be helpful for decision making.

Program evaluation studies have primarily been intended to aid governmental policy makers. One of the most extensive evaluations conducted by the Department of Education has been the National Postsecondary Student Aid Study. Conducted in 1987 and 1990, the study has evaluated student aid and enrollment data for more than sixty thousand students at over one thousand institutions (Korb, Schantz, Stowe, and Zimbler, 1988; Shepard, 1992). These data have been used to determine the efficacy of the federal student aid programs in a wide range of areas. Similarly, other evaluation studies have examined student debt levels, the financial aid delivery system, and institutional and sectorwide compliance with programmatic regulations. However, evaluation studies have not always been well supported by the federal government. As Hearn (1993) notes, several evaluation studies of the federal financial aid programs commissioned by the federal government during the 1970s and 1980s were canceled, underfunded, or diverted to other purposes. In addition, other evaluations by outside sources of the impact of requirements contained in the Drug Free Schools and Communities Act Amendments of 1989 have not been considered by the federal government (Palmer, Gehring, and Guthrie, 1992).

Problem Resolution or Change Phase. The primary goal of the problem resolution phase is program termination. Although it may seem that government is far more proficient at creating new programs than eliminating existing ones, program termination does occasionally happen. Brewer and DeLeon (1983) define termination as "the deliberate conclusion or cessation of specific public sector functions, programs, policies, or organizations" (p. 385). They are also quick to point out that termination often results in the replacement of one program or set of practices with another and that it marks the end as well as the beginning of the policy process.

As noted earlier, the purpose of evaluation should be to determine program efficacy. If evaluation reveals that the program is not meeting its intended goals or that the problems the program was intended to solve are no longer problems, then programs should be terminated. However, there are often as many barriers to termination as there are parties who are invested in the continuation of the program. The barriers include institutional/structural issues, political aspects, economic concerns, psychological impediments, ethical and moral issues, ideological/mythical issues, and legal considerations (Brewer and DeLeon, 1983). Some or all of these issues must be taken into consideration when policy makers decide to terminate a program, and the weight of these demands frequently results in program continuation instead of termination (DeLeon, 1987). Because of the nature of American government, it is frequently easier to start a new program to address an old issue than to eliminate an existing program.

Holistic Policy Development. The Jones model has particular heuristic value, but, like most models attempting to describe complex sociological and political processes, it is overly simplistic, reductionistic, and linear (Kuh, Whitt, and Shedd, 1987). In reality, phases of the policy process overlap, systems interact, and functional processes occur throughout the entire policy cycle. Take, for example, the process of problem definition. In Jones's model, problem definition occurs early in the policy process (shortly after a problem is identified), but in reality problems are defined and redefined during all phases of the process. Indeed, problems may never be defined clearly. The generation of programmatic alternatives and the selection of specific interventions force policy makers to continue the definitional process. An important aspect of program implementation is definition. Bureaucrats (and campus administrators) charged with delivering services to clients frequently have considerable latitude in determining how those services are provided and even which clients are served (Ripley and Franklin, 1986; Lipsky, 1980). It is through these activities that problems are defined and redefined.

Policy Mechanisms

Our national system of government is based on the separation of powers. However, when it comes to policy making, all the branches of government are involved (Kelman, 1987; Ripley and Franklin, 1986). Therefore, the old adage, "The president proposes and Congress disposes" may be a simplistic and inaccurate picture of the policy process.

The Executive Branch. The executive branch's policy-making activities tend to focus on problem identification and program implementation. Through a variety of mechanisms, including the federal budget process and executive orders, the executive branch identifies and defines problems and seeks to propose solutions to problems legitimized through the legislative process. Even at the height of the Reagan years, when the characteristic stance of the executive branch was to reduce federalism, numerous policies were proposed by the executive branch. Although these policies frequently focused on reducing the size of government through the elimination of programs like State Student Incentive Grants and the disestablishment of the Department of Education (Clark and Amiot, 1981), they were policies nonetheless.

The executive branch, through agency oversight and bureaucratic involvement, plays a critical role in the implementation of public policy. Ripley and Franklin (1986) note that "bureaucracies are dominant in the implementation of programs and policies and have varying degrees of importance in other stages of the policy process" (p. 33). With the creation of the Department of Education in 1979, education was granted cabinet-level status in U.S. government. Although the needs of education had been addressed by the federal government before then, the creation of a cabinet-level department formalized education as an important policy-making arena. At the time of its creation, the Department of Education (DE) encompassed over 150 programs. It became the fifth-largest department with the eight-largest budget in the federal government ("Education Policy . . . ," 1981).

Like all governmental bureaucracies, DE plays a number of roles in the policy-making process. These include the following: (1) the provision of services to clients, including individual students and their families, institutions, and other levels of government; (2) the development, distribution, and interpretation of programmatic rules and regulations; (3) policy analysis and program evaluation; (4) data collection; and (5) compliance reviews of campus programmatic activities. In Chapter Six, Gehring will reflect further on the role of the executive branch in implementing and directing campus programs and activities.

The Legislative Branch. For the past twenty years, Congress has played the dominant role in shaping federal higher education policy (Coomes, 1987). Congress tends to focus on problem identification and program evaluation, but as noted earlier, it also plays an important role in program evaluation.

Congress's formulation, legitimation, and appropriation activities are familiar to most as the legislative process. The process begins with the introduction of bills in both chambers of Congress. The bills are referred to the appropriate subcommittees (for example, House Committee on Education and Labor, Subcommittee on Postsecondary Education) for hearings and recommended passage. If these subcommittees pass the identified bills, the bills are forwarded to the full House and Senate for debate and passage. Because few pieces of legislation originating in both chambers are identical, the two versions of a bill must be reconciled in conference committee. These House and Senate conference committees must develop identical pieces of legislation that can be sent back to each chamber for further consideration. The revised legislation, once approved by the House of Representatives and the Senate, is forwarded to the president for signature into law (Oleszek, 1984). Until the final legislation is submitted to both houses by the conference committee, the legislation can be modified and interested parties can influence the shape of final legislation. Once final legislation becomes law, primary responsibility for program implementation is turned over to the appropriate administrative agency.

Although Congress does not implement policy, it has an important role in the program evaluation process through oversight responsibilities. Congressional oversight takes a number of forms, including providing administrative agencies with directions on how policies are to be implemented and retaining the right to comment on regulations developed by administrative agencies. It is not uncommon for members of Congress to request that regulations be modified to reflect more accurately congressional intent or to mandate the withdrawal of regulations inconsistent with that intent. Congress frequently modifies policy through technical amendments, which are changes to existing legislation (particularly large omnibus bills like the 1992 Higher Education Act) that are needed to address issues raised after the bill was passed or to provide further guidance for those implementing the legislation.

Congressional programmatic evaluation can be instigated either through regularly scheduled legislative activities (for example, the five-year reauthorization process of the Higher Education Act 1965) or through the interest of individual members who wish to examine a program's effectiveness. An example of the latter took place in 1990 when the Senate's Permanent Subcommittee on Investigations examined abuses in the Guaranteed Student Loan Program. Although not normally involved in shaping higher education policy (this is the purview of Senate Subcommittee on Education, Arts, and the Humanities), this committee's examination of fraud and abuse shaped discussions of the GSL program during reauthorization.

The Judicial Branch. Court decisions like *Dixon v. Alabama State Board of Education* (1961), *Grove City College v. Bell* (1984), and others have had far-reaching implications for postsecondary education. As Ripley and Franklin (1986) note, "Courts often get deeply involved in implementation questions, not just in the sense of making decisions that limit or channel or mandate certain kinds of implementation, but in the sense that judges and their appointees literally become program administrators" (p. 19). As Kelman (1987) points out, the courts influence and shape policy in a number of ways, including the following: (1) the development of "judge-made 'common law' rules that have grown up alongside laws legislatures pass. Common law rules, mostly of contract and tort law, regulate interactions among private citizens and are an important part of how government has an impact on people's lives" (p. 114) (for example, *Steinberg v. University of Health Sciences/Chicago Medical School,* 1976); (2) the interpretation of the laws passed by Congress (for example, *Grove City College v. Bell,* 1984); (3) the adjudication of decisions made by administrative agencies; and (4) the Supreme Court's authority for judicial review, which allows it not only to declare a law unconstitutional and void but also to rule that "the Constitution requires certain choices" (p. 115). Because each of these judicial functions requires more elaborate discussion than space permits, readers are referred to Kelman (1987) and Horowitz (1977) for a more detailed discussion.

Shaping the Policy Process:
A Role for Student Affairs Professionals

Guba and Lincoln (1981) define stakeholders as groups of people, or individuals, who have a stake in the outcomes of a policy. For the purposes of this discussion, stakeholders are any person, group of persons, or organizations that will be affected by a policy. The stakeholders involved in federal postsecondary education policy are legion: students (and their parents), college faculty, campus administrators, state legislators, federal administrative agency personnel, professional associations like the National Association of Student Financial Aid Administrators (NASFAA). They even include policy makers in the Executive Branch and Congress. (For example, Senator Claiborne Pell, whose name has been attached to the largest federal grant-in-aid program, has a very real stake in seeing that the program remains viable.) It is incumbent upon stakeholders to be diligent in protecting their own interests, and in the case of campus administrators, the interests of the college. College administrators who hope to reap the benefits of participating in federal postsecondary education programs, or who, conversely, want to avoid further entangling their institution with the federal government have a responsibility to participate actively in the process that results in public policy. A woman athlete guaranteed rights under Title IX provisions, a parent participating in the Federal PLUS loan program, or the campus Equal Employment Opportunity Officer responsible for implementing the provisions of the Americans with Disabilities Act all have the responsibility as stakeholders to make sure that their stake in the programs and the process is protected.

The development of policy is a dynamic process, involving multiple actors and stakeholders, played out through a variety of mechanisms. Because of its complex nature, the policy process is frequently misunderstood, and that misunderstanding may prevent relevant stakeholders from participating in the process. It is hoped that this chapter's discussion has sufficiently demystified the policy process for campus stakeholders that they no longer feel inadequately prepared to play a role in shaping policy. Although the complex nature of the process may be confusing, that same complexity provides those who wish to participate in the process with multiple points of entry into the system. Furthermore, the participative nature of our form of government encourages grass-roots efforts to set policy agenda and shape policy outcomes.

Student affairs administrators have an important ethical responsibility to help formulate and implement policies that are in the best interest of their students and institutions. Similarly, they have an equally compelling responsibility to try to change or eliminate federal interventions that will have deleterious effects on institutions and students. The diligent administrator should take advantage of as many of the points of entry into the policy-making process as possible. From the outset, the campus administrator can influence the process by identifying problems and issues that should be addressed. This definitional activity, although highly subjective, is of critical importance because it shapes alternative solutions to the problem that will be considered in the latter stages in the policy formation process. As the most recent reauthorization of the Higher Education Act of 1965 demonstrated in technical policy arenas for example, reforming student aid needs analysis procedures), expertise is important political capital. Student affairs professionals are the acknowledged experts on student life and the impact on it of campus conditions, policies, and environments. As such, they should utilize their expertise to assist governmental policy makers to identify issues clearly, develop appropriate programs, establish guidelines for program implementation, and evaluate program outcomes. Because federal intervention in postsecondary education continues to grow, administrators who can assume the roles of policy analysts and policy makers will become increasingly important to both their institutions and their students.

References

Anderson, J. E. *Public Policy Making.* New York: Praeger, 1975.

Bhola, H. S. "The Design of (Educational) Policy: Directing and Harnessing Social Power for Social Outcomes." Educational Policy: Design, Analysis, Interfaces. *Viewpoints: Bulletin of the School of Education.* Indiana University, Bloomington, May 1975, *51*(3), 1–16.

Bloland, H. G. *Associations in Action: The Washington, D.C., Higher Education Community.* ASHE-ERIC Higher Education Reports, No. 2. Washington, D.C.: George Washington University, 1985.

Brewer, G., and DeLeon, P. *The Foundations of Policy Analysis.* Homewood, Ill.: Dorsey Press, 1983.

Bull, B. "A Conception of Policy and Its Implication for Policy Study." Unpublished manuscript, Indiana University, Bloomington, n d.

Clark, D. L., and Amiot, M. A. "The Impact of the Reagan Administration on Federal Education Policy." *The Phi Delta Kappan,* December 1981, *63,* 258–262.

Cobb, R. W., and Elder, C.D. *Participation in American Politics: The Dynamics of Agenda-Building.* Boston: Allyn and Bacon, 1972.

Coomes, M. D. "An Examination of Changes in Federal Student Financial Aid Policy from 1981 to 1985–1986." Unpublished doctoral dissertation, School of Education, Indiana University, Bloomington, 1987.

Cronbach, L. J., Ambron, S. R., Dornbusch, S. M., Hess, R. D., Hornik, R. C., Phillips, D. C., Walker, D. F., and Weiner, S. S. *Toward Reform of Program Evaluation: Aims, Methods, and Institutional Arrangements.* San Francisco: Jossey-Bass, 1980.

DeLeon, P. "Policy Termination as a Political Phenomenon." In D. J. Palumbo (ed.), *The Politics of Program Evaluation.* Vol. 15. *Sage Yearbooks in Politics and Public Policy.* Newbury Park, Calif.: Sage, 1987.

DeLoughry, T. J. "College Officials Say Politics and Budgetary Constraints Have Doomed Reauthorization Bill's Promise of Reform." *Chronicle of Higher Education,* Apr. 22, 1992, pp. A29, A34–A35.

"Education Policy: Chronology of Action on Education." *Congress and the Nation: A Review of Government and Politics Vol. V, 1977–1980.* Washington, D.C.: Congressional Quarterly, 1981.

General Accounting Office. *HRD-91–4BR Education Regulations.* Washington, D.C.: General Accounting Office, Nov. 15, 1990.

Gergen, K. J. "Assessing the Leverage Points in the Process of Policy Formulation." In R. A. Bauer and K. J. Gergen (eds.), *The Study of Policy Formation.* New York: Free Press, 1968.

Gilbert, G. R. "The Study of Policy Formulation and Conduct of Policy Analysis and Evaluation." In G. R. Gilbert (ed.), *Making and Managing Public Policy: Formulation, Analysis, Evaluation.* Public Administration and Public Policy, No. 23. New York: Marcel Dekker, 1984.

Gladieux, L. E., and Wolanin, T. R. *Congress and the Colleges.* Lexington, Mass.: Lexington Books, 1976.

Guba, E. G., and Lincoln, Y. S. *Effective Evaluation: Improving the Usefulness of Evaluation Results Through Responsive and Naturalistic Approaches.* San Francisco: Jossey-Bass, 1981.

Hartmark, L. S., and Hines, E. R. "Politics and Policy in Higher Education: Reflections on the Status of the Field." In S. K. Gove and T. M. Stauffer (eds.), *Policy Controversies in Higher Education.* New York: Greenwood Press, 1986.

Hawkins, H. *Banding Together: The Rise of National Associations in American Higher Education, 1887–1950.* Baltimore, Md.: Johns Hopkins University Press, 1992.

Hearn, J. C. "The Paradox of Growth in Federal Aid for College Students, 1965–1990." In J. C. Smart (ed.), *Higher Education: Handbook of Theory and Research.* Vol. 9. New York: Agathon Press, 1993.

Horowitz, D. L. *The Courts and Social Policy.* Washington, D.C.: Brookings Institute, 1977.

Jones, C. O. *An Introduction to the Study of Public Policy.* (2nd ed.) Belmont, Calif.: Wadsworth, 1977.

Jones, C. O., and Matthes, D. "Policy Formulation." In S. S. Nagel (ed.), *Encyclopedia of Policy Studies.* New York: Marcel Dekker, 1983.

Kelman, S. *Making Public Policy: A Hopeful View of American Government.* New York: Basic Books, 1987.

Korb, R., Schantz, N., Stowe, P., and Zimbler, L. *Undergraduate Financing of Postsecondary Education: A Report of the 1987 National Postsecondary Student Aid Study.* Washington, D.C.: National Center for Education Statistics, 1988.

Kuh, G. D., Whitt, E. J., and Shedd, J. D. *Student Affairs Work, 2001: A Paradigmatic Odyssey.* ACPA Media Publication No. 24. Alexandria, Va.: American College Personnel Association, 1987.

Lindbloom, C. E. "The Science of Muddling Through." *Public Administration Review,* 1959, *19,* 79–88.

Lindbloom, C. E. *The Policy Making Process.* Englewood Cliffs, N.J.: Prentice Hall, 1968.

Lindbloom, C. E. "Still Muddling, Not Yet Through." *Public Administration Review,* 1979, *39,* 517–526.

Lipsky, M. *Street-Level Bureaucracy: Dilemmas of the Individual in Public Sectors.* New York: Russell Sage, 1980.

Madaus, G. F., Scrivin, M., and Stufflebeam, D. L. *Evaluation Models: Viewpoints on Educational and Human Services Evaluation.* Boston: Kluwer-Nejhoff, 1988.

Odden, A. R. "The Evolution of Education Policy Implementation." In A. R. Odden (ed.), *Education Policy Implementation.* Albany: State University of New York Press, 1991.

Oleszek, W. J. *Congressional Procedures and the Policy Process.* (2nd ed.) Washington, D.C.: CQ Press, 1984.

Nachmias, D. *Public Policy Evaluation: Approaches and Methods.* New York: St. Martin's Press, 1979.

Palmer, C. J., Gehring, D. D., and Guthrie, V. L. "Student Knowledge of Information Mandated by the 1989 Amendments to the Drug Free Schools and Communities Act." *NASPA Journal,* 1992, *30*(1), 30–42.

Paris, D. C., and Reynolds, J. F. *The Logic of Policy Inquiry.* New York: Longman, 1983.

Pressman, J. L., and Wildavsky, A. *Implementation.* Berkeley: University of California Press, 1973.

Ripley, R. B., and Franklin, G. A. *Policy Implementation and Bureaucracy.* (2nd ed.) Chicago: Dorsey Press, 1986.

Rothschild, M. "Communication Strategy in a Higher Education Social Influence Situation." Unpublished doctoral dissertation, School of Education, Indiana University, Bloomington, 1992.

Rudolph, F. *The American College and University: A History.* Athens: University of Georgia Press, 1990.

Schwartz, P., and Ogilvy, J. *The Emergent Paradigm: Changing Patterns of Thought and Belief.* Analytical Report No. 7, Values and Lifestyles Program. Menlo Park, Calif.: SRI International, 1979.

Shepard, J. (Project Director). *Methodology Report of the 1990 National Postsecondary Student Aid Study: Contractor Report.* Washington, D.C.: National Center for Education Statistics, 1992.

Strange, C. C., and King, P. M. "The Professional Practice of Student Development." In D. G. Creamer and Associates, *College Student Development: Theory and Practice for the 1990s.* American College Personnel Association Media Publication No. 49. Alexandria, Va.: American College Personnel Association, 1990.

White, M. J. "Policy Analysis Models." In S. S. Nagel (ed.), *Encyclopedia of Policy Studies.* New York: Marcel Dekker, 1983.

Wirt, F., and Kirst, M. *Schools in Conflict.* (2nd ed.) Berkeley, Calif.: McCutchan, 1989.
Wise, C. R. *The Dynamics of Legislation: Leadership and Policy Change in the Congressional Process.* San Francisco: Jossey-Bass, 1991.

Cases

Dixon v. Alabama State Board of Education, 294 F.2d 150 (5th Cir., 1961).
Grove City College v. Bell, 194S. Ct. 1211 (1984).
Steinberg v. University of Health Sciences/Chicago Medical School, 42 Ill. App. 3d 804 (354 N.E. 2d 586, 1976).

MICHAEL D. COOMES is assistant professor of higher education and student affairs at Bowling Green State University.

DONALD HOSSLER is chair of the Department of Educational Leadership and Policy Studies and associate professor of higher education and student affairs at Indiana University, Bloomington.

This chapter discusses five antidiscrimination statutes that have significant impact upon institutions of higher education. Cases interpreting the statutes as well as various implications for student affairs practitioners are discussed.

Antidiscrimination Laws and Student Affairs

Timothy A. Bills, Patrick J. Hall

This chapter provides a brief introduction to five federal antidiscrimination laws. A general examination of federal statutes and their relationship to the Constitution is offered as a foundation for understanding statutory relevance in higher education. Although numerous federal statutes have been enacted to safeguard civil rights, this chapter provides an examination of five statutes that have significant impact on student affairs administration in institutions of higher education. The following ones are the focus of this chapter: Title VI of the Civil Rights Act of 1964 (Title VI); Title VII of the Civil Rights Act of 1964 (Title VII); Title IX of the Educational Amendments of 1972 (Title IX); Section 504 of the Rehabilitation Act of 1973 (Section 504); and the Americans with Disabilities Act of 1990 (ADA). As Seaquist (1988) notes, these statutes "affect virtually every aspect of administering a student affairs office" (p. 98). Thus, it is imperative that student affairs professionals have a sound understanding of the rights that students and employees derive from these statutes.

The statutes introduced in this chapter are discussed in light of the Civil Rights Restoration Act of 1987 (P.L. 100–259), which restored the broad institutionwide application of Title VI, Title IX, and Section 504. Although the scope of this chapter does not permit extensive discussion of specific cases related to these statutes, relevant cases are cited throughout.

It should be noted that this chapter is not designed as legal advice. Competent legal counsel should be consulted concerning legal issues, concerns, and policy. This chapter only provides a basic introduction to legal issues in higher education and serves as an impetus for further learning and discussion about them.

Regulations and Guidelines

Antidiscrimination laws or statutes provide general guidance. However, their intent and legal interpretation is better understood through an examination of their regulations and supporting guidelines. When examining civil rights law, student affairs professionals should recognize the difference between regulations and guidelines.

Regulations "are issued to effectuate the intent of statutes . . . . These regulations contain detailed specifications of policies, practices and procedures permitted and precluded by law" (Gehring, 1991, p. 398). The civil rights statutes governing recipients of federal financial assistance delegate enforcement responsibilities to each of the federal agencies disbursing the assistance. These agencies then publish regulations that have the status of law. Thus, postsecondary institutions may be subject to the civil rights regulations of several federal agencies (Kaplin, 1985). For student affairs professionals, the most important regulations are those issued by the Department of Education (DE), which has its own Office of Civil Rights (OCR), under the direction of an assistant secretary for civil rights. The OCR has enforcement responsibilities for Title VI, Title IX, and Section 504. The DE regulations concerning civil rights are published in Volume 34 of the Code of Federal Regulations (C.F.R.), Parts 100–106.

Guidelines are studied interpretations of federal statutes that are offered by administrative agencies pursuant to their interpretive powers. Although both guidelines and regulations are published by federal administrative agencies, guidelines differ from regulations in that they are not implemented with definitive authority from Congress. Thus, guidelines do not have the force and effect of law. However, they are legally significant because they provide guidance to the public and the courts on the correct interpretation of various legal provisions. Often courts show great deference to administrative agency guidelines by adopting their definitions and legal interpretations. For example, in 1980, the Equal Employment Opportunity Commission (EEOC), an administrative agency created under Title VII, issued guidelines defining and addressing sexual harassment. In 1986, the EEOC definition of sexual harassment was adopted by the Supreme Court in its first sexual harassment case under Title VII, *Meritor Savings Bank v. Vinson* (1986). Thus, as Haney (1993) explains, "The EEOC guidelines are not binding on courts but have persuasive weight because they are the official view of the EEOC, the agency charged with the administration of Title VII" (p. 1038). The EEOC guidelines for Title VII are published in the Code of Federal Regulations. Policy interpretations are similar to guidelines in their legal significance. Policy interpretations offered by the OCR are published in the Federal Register.

Federal Antidiscrimination Statutes and the Constitution

Federal antidiscrimination statutes are laws enacted by Congress to prohibit discrimination in employment, education, professions, or various other segments of our society. As Barr (1988) notes, federal statutes "govern all the citizens of all the states and must be consistent with the powers reserved for the federal government under the United States Constitution" (p. 8). By placing conditions on spending, three of these antidiscrimination statutes (Title VI, Title IX, and Section 504) represent an exercise of congressional spending power under Article I § 8 of the Constitution, achieved through the delegation of authority by Congress "to the various federal departments and agencies that administer federal aid programs" (Kaplin, 1985, p. 517). Additional justification for the enactment of civil rights legislation stems from Congress's power to enforce the Fourteenth Amendment's equal protection clause (U.S. Constitution, Amendment XIV, § 5).

Many legal issues related to discrimination may be presented in both constitutional and statutory terms. Similarities exist between the rights guaranteed by the Fourteenth Amendment's equal protection clause and the protections against discrimination enumerated in federal statutes and their enabling regulations. Antidiscrimination statutory law "parallels and in some ways is more protective than the equal protection principles derived from the Fourteenth Amendment" (Kaplin, 1985, p. 25). Thus, "in some instances, statutes and regulations implementing them set higher standards than do constitutional rights" (Gehring, 1991, p. 397). Gehring supported this assertion with this example: "A curfew for female students without a corresponding restriction for men was upheld under the 'rational relationship' test for equal protection under the Fourteenth Amendment [citing *Robinson v. Eastern Kentucky University* (1973)]. This same rule, however, would violate a student's statutory rights, as defined by federal regulations, under Title IX [34 C.F.R. 106]" (p. 397–398).

Student affairs professionals should understand the similarities and differences between constitutional and statutory relationships, especially in terms of their applicability, legal standards, scope, and coverage.

Application. "The Constitution of the United States provides in its amendments certain rights that guarantee citizens protection against certain actions by the government or its agencies" (Gehring; 1991, p. 381). As agencies of the government, state-supported colleges and universities must uphold the rights guaranteed students and employees under both the U.S. Constitution and state constitutions. However, the Constitution does not provide protection against purely private conduct. Thus, at private colleges, the rights of members of the academic community are not protected by the Constitution unless the private institution is engaged in "state action," meaning that the private institution is so entwined with the government that its actions are essentially those of the government. "The concept of a private institution being involved in state action has seldom been applied by the courts" (Gehring, 1991, p. 381). The mere receipt of funding from the government (whether state or federal) has not been enough to bring colleges within the rubric of state action. When allegations of racial discrimination have been involved, however, courts have shown increased scrutiny in determining the existence of state action (see *Burton v. Wilmington Parking Authority,* 1961).

Although they are not required to protect constitutional rights, private institutions usually uphold constitutional safeguards through rules and regulations that form a contractual relationship between the institution and its faculty, staff, and students. Further, Title VI of the Civil Rights Act of 1964, Title IX of the Educational Amendments of 1972, and Section 504 of the Rehabilitation Act of 1973 prohibit discrimination in any program or activity receiving federal financial assistance. Kaplin (1985) cautioned that "although the language of these statutes is similar, each statute protects a different group of beneficiaries, and an act that constitutes discrimination against one group does not necessarily constitute discrimination against another group" (p. 517). However, the application of these statutes to higher education institutions was made consistent by amendments enacted as part of the Civil Rights Restoration Act of 1987 (P.L. 100–259). Before that year, uncertainty about the definition of "program and activity" and its interrelationship to the phrase "receiving federal financial assistance" resulted in substantial legal debate over the scope of the antidiscrimination statutes (Kaplin, 1985). The courts were confronted with numerous questions about the concepts of program or activity. The legal debate culminated in *Grove City v. Bell* (1984), a Title IX gender discrimination case involving the financial aid office of a private college. In *Grove City v. Bell,* the Supreme Court made two important rulings: (a) student receipt of federal financial aid constituted federal financial assistance to the college under Title IX, thus making the institution a "recipient"; and (b) the receipt of federal financial assistance by the college's financial aid program did not trigger institutionwide coverage under Title IX but, instead, held only the financial aid program accountable to Title IX regulations and sanctions. Thus, under the Court's ruling a college or university that discriminated against women, for example, could continue to receive federal funding if that discrimination was not involved in a federally funded program.

The second part of the *Grove City* decision was criticized by members of Congress, who argued that the narrow application of the statute was (a) inconsistent with the legislation's congressional intent and (b) symbolic of a weakening commitment to civil rights under the Reagan administration. Less than two months after the ruling, a bipartisan coalition in Congress introduced legislation "to restore the broad scope of coverage and to clarify the application of [federal antidiscrimination statutes]" (Civil Rights Restoration Act of 1987, P.L. 100–259). After continuing debate, a three-year struggle, and the veto of President Reagan, the legislation was enacted as the Civil Rights Restoration Act of 1987, which amended Title VI, Title IX, and Section 504 to define "program or activity" as "all of the operations of a college, university, or other postsecondary institution, or a public system of higher education" (P.L. 100–259).

Viewed together, the *Grove City* analysis and the Civil Rights Restoration Act of 1987 provide a clear definition of the concepts "recipient of federal financial assistance" and "program or activity." An institution is considered a "recipient of federal assistance" if it (a) receives federal aid directly (for example, construction grants, property, services, or research contracts) or (b) receives federal financial assistance indirectly through student financial aid. (See Title IX regulations at 34 C.F.R. § 106.2(g) for a more detailed definition of federal financial assistance.) "Program or activity" is defined to include all operations of a college or university. Thus, Title VI, Title IX, and Section 504 apply to all operations of virtually all public and private institutions. If an institution is a recipient of any amount of federal financial assistance in any program, the entire institution is subject to the prohibitions against discrimination enumerated by these civil rights statutes. Conversely, if discrimination is proven in any institutional program, all of the institution's federal funds are at risk.

Title VI of the Civil Rights Act of 1964

Title VI of the Civil Rights Act of 1964 (see Appendix) proclaims: "No person in the United States shall, on the ground of race, color, or national origin, be excluded from participation in, be denied the benefits of, or be subjected to discrimination under any program or activity receiving Federal financial assistance."

Title VI is accompanied by lengthy enabling regulations (found at 34 C.F.R. §§ 100.1–100.13) that explain the law in more detail. Examples of discriminatory acts expressly prohibited by the statute are provided in Section 100.3(b) of the DE regulations for Title VI. These regulations state that a recipient of federal funds "may not, directly or through contractual or other arrangements, on [the] ground[s] of race, color, or national origin:

i   Deny an individual any service, financial aid, or other benefit provided under the program;

ii Provide any service, financial aid, or other benefit to an individual which is different, or is provided in a different manner, from that provided to others under the program;

iii Subject an individual to segregation or separate treatment in any matter related to his receipt of any service, financial aid, or other benefit under the program;

iv Restrict an individual in any way in the enjoyment of any advantage or privilege enjoyed by others receiving any service, financial aid, or other benefit under the program;

v   Treat an individual differently from others in determining whether he satisfies any admission, enrollment, quota, eligibility, membership or other requirement or condition which individuals must meet in order to be provided any service, financial aid, or other benefit provided under the program;

vi Deny an individual an opportunity to participate in the program through the provision of services or otherwise or afford him an opportunity to do so which is different from that afforded others under the program (including the opportunity to participate in the program as an employee but only to the extent set forth in paragraph (c) of this section); [or]

vii Deny a person the opportunity to participate as a member of a planning or advisory body which is an integral part of the program."

Coverage. As a condition of receiving federal financial assistance, institutions must file documents with the federal government assuring that the program will be conducted or that the facility operates in compliance with all requirements. Student affairs administrators should be aware that "in the case of any application for Federal financial assistance to an institution of higher education (including assistance for construction, for research, for a special training project, for student loans or for any other purpose), the assurance required shall extend to admission practices and to all other practices relating to the treatment of students" (34 C.F.R. § 100.4 (d) (1)). Thus, regulations make clear that discriminatory practices in admissions are expressly prohibited.

Institutions must keep records and submit to the responsible DE official complete and accurate reports as deemed necessary by the DE to determine compliance. In addition, as a condition of receiving federal financial assistance, institutions of higher education are subject to compliance investigations. Therefore, they "should have available for the Department [of Education] racial and ethnic data showing the extent to which members of minority groups are beneficiaries of and participants in federally assisted programs" (34 C.F.R. § 100.6[b]). Institutions must "permit access by [the DE] during normal business hours to . . . its books, records, accounts, and any other sources of information, and its facilities as may be pertinent to ascertain compliance" (34 C.F.R. § 100.6[c]). The DE will "from time to time review the practices of recipients to determine whether they are complying" (34 C.F.R. § 100.7[a]).

Complaints. Persons who believe that they or any specific class of individuals have been subjected to discrimination may file a written complaint with the DE's Office of Civil Rights. Complaints must be filed not later than 180 days from the date of the alleged discrimination, unless an extension is granted by the responsible department official or a designee. If a complaint has been filed, DE investigations should include a review of the pertinent practices and policies of the institution, the circumstances under which the alleged noncompliance occurred, and other factors relevant to noncompliance. If it is ruled that an institution is in violation of compliance, the DE will inform the recipient and the matter will be resolved by informal means whenever possible. If it is determined that the matter cannot be resolved through informal means, further action will be taken. Further action may include any of the following three steps: (a) suspension or termination of or refusal to grant federal financial assistance; (b) referral to the Department of Justice for judicial proceedings; (c) any applicable proceeding under state or local law. Termination of or refusal to grant or continue federal financial assistance will not occur until (a) the DE has advised the institution of its failure to comply and determined that voluntary means for compliance cannot be secured; (b) there has been an express finding on record, after opportunity for hearing, of a failure by the applicant or recipient to comply with a requirement imposed by or pursuant to this part; (c) thirty days has expired after the Secretary of Education has filed with the appropriate congressional committees a full written report of the circumstances involved and the grounds for such action (see 34 C.F.R. § 100.7 § 100.8 [a]).

The regulations also prohibit intimidatory or retaliatory acts against any individual in response to his or her filing of a complaint or involvement in any investigation, proceeding, or hearing related to Title VI. Confidentiality is to be kept "except to the extent necessary to carry out . . . the conduct of any investigation, hearing, or judicial proceeding arising thereunder" (34 C.F.R. § 100.7 [e]).

Title VII of the Civil Rights Act of 1964

Title VII evolved out of a bill that was proposed by the Kennedy administration in 1963 and was originally intended to protect African Americans from racial discrimination in employment. After extensive amendments by the House Judiciary Committee, the bill was reported to the House of Representatives, where it again was amended. One of the amendments, offered by an opponent of the entire Civil Rights Act in an apparent attempt to defeat the bill, incorporated protection on the basis of sex. This important amendment was accepted with little debate and the bill eventually passed Congress and was signed into law by President Johnson as part of the Civil Rights Act of 1964 (Player, Shoben, and Lieberwitz, 1992, pp. 16–17).

Coverage. Now considered "the most comprehensive and most litigated of the federal employment discrimination laws" (Kaplin, 1985, p. 121), Title VII of the Civil Rights Act of 1964 made it . . . an unlawful employment practice for an employer

1. To fail or refuse to hire or to discharge any individual, or otherwise to discriminate against any individual with respect to his compensation, terms, conditions, or privileges of employment, because of such individual's race, color, religion, sex, or national origin; or
2. To limit, segregate, or classify his employees or applicants for employment in any way which would deprive or tend to deprive any individual of employment opportunities or otherwise adversely affect his status as an employee, because of such individual's race, color, religion, sex, or national origin (42 U.S.C. § 2000e–2[a]).

One major exception that is enumerated as part of the statute is the bona fide occupational qualification (BFOQ) standard, which states that hiring and employing practices based upon "religion, sex, or national origin" are permissible when such a characteristic is a "bona fide occupational qualification necessary to the normal operation of that particular business or enterprise" (42 U.S.C. § 2000e–2[e] [1]). Thus, it would not violate Title VII for a

Methodist-affiliated institution, for example, to consider only Methodist ministers for the position of campus minister, because that would be a bona fide occupational qualification for that position.

There is no BFOQ for race. However, Congress indicated that authenticity could justify national origin discrimination (110 Cong. Rec. 7317). Authenticity may also be considered in permitting discrimination based on gender. The EEOC guidelines state that "where it is necessary for the purpose of authenticity or genuineness, the Commission will consider sex to be a bona fide occupational qualification, e.g., an actor or actress" (29 C.F.R. § 1604.2, 1989). In addition to the broad BFOQ applicable to religious distinctions, Title VII provided the following:

> [I]t shall not be an unlawful employment practice for a school, college, university, or other educational institution or institution of learning to hire and employ employees of a particular religion, if such . . . institution is, in whole or substantial part, owned, supported, controlled, or managed by a particular religious corporation, association, or society, or if the curriculum of such . . . institution is directed toward the propagation of a particular religion (42 U.S.C. § 2000e–2[e] [2]).

An additional exception was stipulated in regard to Native Americans and their reservations:

> Nothing contained in this title shall apply to any business or enterprise on or near an Indian reservation with respect to any publicly announced employment practice of such business or enterprise under which a preferential treatment is given to any individual because he is an Indian living on or near a reservation (42 U.S.C. § 2000e–2[i]).

Thus, it is permissible for postsecondary institutions located on or near reservations to discriminate in favor of Native Americans in employment practices.

Other employment practices prohibited by the statute include the following: (a) discrimination against anyone because he or she opposed any practice made unlawful by Title VII or because he or she made a charge, testified, assisted, or participated in any manner in an investigation, proceeding, or hearing under this title (see 42 U.S.C. § 2000e–3[a]); and (b) publishing any notice or advertisement relating to employment . . . indicating any preference, limitation, specification, or discrimination, based on race, color, religion, sex, or national origin, except when such notice is based upon a bona fide occupational qualification for employment (see 42 U.S.C. § 2000e–3[b]). Generally, under Title VII, "institutions retain discretion to hire, promote, reward, and terminate faculty as they choose, as long as they do not make distinctions based on race, color, religion, sex, or national origin" (Kaplin, 1985, p. 121).

The Equal Employment Opportunity Act of 1972 made extensive coverage and procedural amendments to the 1964 act, including the extension of

Title VII for the first time to state governments, local governments, and public and private educational institutions. It also reduced the number of employees necessary for an institution to fall within the mandates of Title VII. In 1972, the definition of "religion" was expanded to include "religious practices" and imposed upon employers the obligation to make "reasonable accommodation" to such religious practices.

The Pregnancy Discrimination Amendments of 1978, which were the result of congressional reaction to the Supreme Court ruling in *General Electric Co. v. Gilbert* (1976), added § 701(k) that defined "sex" to include "pregnancy, childbirth, or related medical conditions," and required employers to treat pregnancy and childbirth as they did as other conditions similarly affecting the ability to work. In interpreting "sex" to refer only to gender, the courts have ruled that distinctions based on sexual practices and sexual orientations are not protected by Title VII (see *DeSantis v. Pacific Tel. and Tel. Co.,* 1979).

"[T]he language of Title VII is not limited to 'economic' or 'tangible' discrimination. The phrase 'terms, conditions, or privileges of employment' evinces a congressional intent 'to strike at the entire spectrum of disparate treatment' "(*Meritor Savings Bank v. Vinson* [1986]). In *Meritor,* sexual harassment did not result in the loss of the job or income; nonetheless, it stated a Title VII claim. In addition, Title VII prohibits discrimination in any apprenticeship, training, retraining or on-the-job training program (§ 703[d]).

Complaints. Executive Orders 12067 and 12106 established the Equal Employment Opportunity Commission (EEOC) to coordinate the efforts of federal agencies in enforcing federal statutes designed to eliminate discrimination in employment and enforce equal employment programs. Employees who believe that they have been discriminated against on the basis of race, color, religion, sex, national origin, age, or disability may file complaints with EEOC, which conducts an investigation into the allegations. Individuals may also bring suits in federal courts to enforce their rights guaranteed under Title VII.

Title IX of the Educational Amendments of 1972

Title IX of the Educational Amendments of 1972 (see Appendix) declares that "No person in the United States shall, on the basis of sex, be excluded from participation in, be denied the benefits of, or be subjected to discrimination under any education program or activity receiving Federal financial assistance" (20 U.S.C. § 1681).

Generally stated, Title IX prohibits discrimination on the basis of sex in public and private educational institutions that receive federal funds. The Department of Education's Office of Civil Rights is responsible for ensuring compliance.

Coverage. Unlike Title VI, Title IX is limited to educational programs receiving federal financial assistance. In regard to admissions to educational institutions, Title IX applies "only to institutions of vocational education, professional education, and graduate higher education, and to public institutions of undergraduate higher education" (20 U.S.C. § 1681 [a] [1]). Thus, the admissions practices of private undergraduate institutions are exempt from Title IX.

Title IX enumerates several exceptions by stating that it shall not apply to

a An educational institution which is controlled by a religious organization if the application of this subsection would not be consistent with the religious tenets of such organization (20 U.S.C. § 1681 [a] [3]);
b An educational institution whose primary purpose is the training of individuals for the military services of the United States, or the merchant marine (20 U.S.C. § 1681 [a] [4])
c In regard to admissions . . . any public institution of undergraduate higher education which is an institution that traditionally and continually from its establishment has had a policy of admitting only students of one sex (20 U.S.C. § 1681 [a] [5]);
d Membership practices of a social fraternity or social sorority which is exempt from taxation under section 501(a) of the Internal Revenue Code of 1954 (26 U.S.C. § 501 [a]), the active membership of which consists primarily of students in attendance at an institution of higher education (20 U.S.C. § 1681 [a] [6] [A]);
e Membership practices of the YMCA, YWCA, Girl Scouts, Boy Scouts, Camp Fire Girls, and voluntary youth service organizations provided the membership has traditionally been limited to persons of one sex and principally to persons of less than nineteen years of age (20 U.S.C. § 1681 [a] [6] [B]);
f Boy or girl conferences associated with the American Legion including Boys State, Girls State, Boys Nation, and Girls Nation (20 U.S.C. § 1681 [a] [7]);
g Father-son or mother-daughter activities at educational institutions (20 U.S.C. § 1681 [a] [8]); and
h Institutions of higher education in regard to scholarships awarded in beauty pageants (20 U.S.C. § 1681 [a] [9]).

The DE's regulations for effectuating Title IX provide general and specific prohibitions pursuant to the statute. These prohibitions are presented in regard to admissions, recruitment, educational programs and activities, and employment. These provisions are directly applicable to student affairs administrators and should be made familiar to student affairs staff members.

Admissions. Subpart C of the DE's Title IX regulations prohibits discrimination on the basis of sex in admissions and recruitment (see 34 C.F.R. §§ 106.21–106.23). Prohibited acts include treating one individual differently from another on the basis of sex, including (a) giving a person preference on the basis of sex by ranking applicants separately on such basis and (b) applying numerical limitations on the number or proportion of persons of either sex who may be admitted. Preference in admission cannot be given based on an individual's previous attendance at an educational institution or other school that admits students only or predominantly of one sex. Similarly, predominant or exclusive recruitment at institutions is prohibited if such actions have the effect of discriminating on the basis of sex. Admissions tests that have a disproportionate adverse effect on persons of one sex are also prohibited unless (a) they can be shown to validly predict success and (b) alternative tests without such disproportionate effects are unavailable. Discrimination based on family, parental, or marital status, as well as on pregnancy, childbirth, termination of pregnancy, or recovery therefrom is also prohibited. Preadmission inquiries regarding the sex of candidates are permissible provided that the questions are asked of all candidates and that the results of such inquiries are not used in a discriminatory manner. The prohibitions related to nondiscrimination in admission do not apply to private institutions of undergraduate education (34 C.F.R. § 86.15 [d]).

Student Fees and Financial Aid. Title IX regulations prohibit the following acts on the basis of sex (a) the denial, differential provision, or provision in a different manner of any aid, benefit, or service (34 C.F.R. § 106.31 [b] [2–3]); and (b) the application of "any rule concerning the domicile or residence of a student or applicant, including eligibility for in-state fees and tuition" (34 C.F.R. § 106.31 [b] [5]).

Community Service/Off-Campus Housing. A provision against aiding or perpetuating the "discrimination against any person by providing significant assistance to any agency, organization, or person which discriminates on the basis of sex in providing any aid, benefit or service to students or employees" (34 C.F.R. § 106.31 [b] [6]) provokes implications for a number of student affairs functional areas including volunteer programs and off-campus housing offices.

International Programs. Generally, an institution is permitted to administer or assist in the administration of scholarships, fellowships, or other awards restricted on the basis of sex that have been established by foreign or domestic wills or trusts, or acts of foreign governments that are designed to provide opportunities for study abroad, provided they make available reasonable opportunities for similar studies for members of the opposite sex (34 C.F.R. § 106.31 [c]).

Housing and Judicial Affairs. Title IX prohibits, on the basis of sex, the application of different rules or regulations, the imposition of different fees or requirements, and the offering of different services or benefits related to housing (with some exceptions, including married student housing) (34 C.F.R. § 106.32 [a]). Separate housing on the basis of sex is permissible provided that it is (a) comparable in quality and cost and (b) proportionate in quantity based on the number of students of that sex applying for such housing (34 C.F.R. § 106.32 [b] [1–2]). In other words, toilets, showers, and locker rooms must be comparable. Similarly, in the area of judicial affairs Title IX prohibits subjecting any student, on the basis of sex, to separate or different rules of behavior, sanctions, or other treatments (34 C.F.R. § 106.31 [b] [4]).

Athletics. Discrimination on the basis of sex is also prohibited in athletics

(34 C.F.R. § 86.14). However, institutions may have separate teams for members of each sex "where selection for such teams is based upon competitive skills or the activity is a contact sport." When the institution operates teams for one sex and not the other, except for boxing, football, basketball, wrestling, rugby, ice hockey, and other contact sports, those excluded must be given the choice to try out for the sport if the opportunity to participate in that sport has been limited in the past. Factors considered in determining whether there is discrimination include provision of equipment and supplies, scheduling of games and practices, travel and per diem allowances, coaching and tutoring opportunities, the assignment and compensation of coaches and tutors, facilities, medical and training services, housing and dining facilities and services and publicity. Student affairs staff responsible for intercollegiate athletics should also be aware of and familiar with the government's policy interpretation related to Title IX and intercollegiate athletics appear-ing at 44 Fed. Reg. 71413 (Dec. 11, 1979), which expands upon the criteria listed here.

Complaints. A private right of action exists under Title IX. This essentially means that individuals may bring suits to enforce their rights under the act. Complaints may also be made to the Office of Civil Rights of the Department of Education, which will investigate and attempt voluntary compliance if violation is found. The compliance procedures for Title IX are the same as those for Title VI.

Section 504 of the Rehabilitation Act of 1973

Section 504 of the Rehabilitation Act of 1973 was enacted by the United States Congress to provide protection for handicapped persons against various forms of societal discrimination. Popularly known today as simply "Section 504," this legislation has had a significant impact on the overall operation of higher education and the various relationships that individual institutions have with handicapped persons. It is crucial for leaders within the higher education community to have a working knowledge of their individual and institutional obligations under Section 504 in order to promote a supportive and accessible educational environment for all persons and to protect their limited resources from claims of illegal discrimination.

Coverage. Section 504, as amended and now appearing at 29 USC §794, provides in pertinent part that "No otherwise qualified individual with handicaps in the United States . . . shall, solely by reason of her or his handicap, be excluded from the participation in, be denied the benefits of, or be subjected to discrimination under any program or activity receiving Federal financial assistance." The federal regulations implementing Section 504 provide that the act applies to every recipient of funds from the DE and "to each program or activity that receives or benefits from such assistance" (34 C.F.R. § 104.2). Recalling the earlier discussion of the impact of the Civil Rights Restoration Act of 1987 and the *Grove City* case (regarding the expansive definitions of "recipients of financial assistance" and "program or activity"), one can see that every program or activity at nearly every college and university in the United States must comply with Section 504.

Section 504 provides that all institutions that apply for federal financial assistance must submit an assurance form to the DE certifying that they will comply with the act. It further requires institutions to designate an employee to be responsible for coordinating compliance with the act, and for adopting grievance procedures for handling alleged violations. Institutions must also provide continuing notice to employees (current and prospective), students, and applicants that they do not discriminate on the basis of handicap. The notice must identify the responsible employee for coordinating compliance and be included in recruitment materials used by the institution. The act also suggests that institutions may post notices in buildings and place them in campus publications such as newspapers and magazines.

In delineating who is covered as "handicapped persons" under Section 504, the act is also very broad in scope. It includes "any person who (i) has a physical or mental impairment which substantially limits one or more major life activities, (ii) has a record of such an impairment, or (iii) is regarded as having such an impairment" (34 C.F.R. § 104.3 [j] [1]). It thus includes persons who have easily verifiable impairments (for example, deafness or blindness) as well as those who are treated by a recipient as though they have an impairment even if it is not something normally considered a handicap (such as a person with a limp or disfiguring scars). In any case, to qualify, a person's physical or mental impairment (or recipient's treatment) must be such that it substantially limits one or more of their "major life activities . . . such as caring for one's self, performing manual tasks, walking, seeing, hearing, speaking, breathing, learning, and working" (34 C.F.R. § 104.4 [j] [2] [ii]). Although it does not provide a comprehensive list of handicaps that qualify, the DE pointed out in its analysis of Section 504 that it includes specific learning disabilities (for example, brain injury and dyslexia) and "such diseases and conditions as orthopedic, visual, speech, and hearing impediments, cerebral palsy, epilepsy, muscular dystrophy, multiple sclerosis, cancer, heart disease, diabetes, mental retardation, emotional illness, . . . drug addiction and alcoholism" (34 C.F.R. § 104 Appendix A, Subpart A[3]). With regard to drug addiction and alcoholism and their relationship to employment, it is important to point out that although drug addicts and alcoholics may not be discriminated against solely on the basis of their condition, their work performance can be judged on the same basis as for other employees. Thus if the condition has a negative effect on the person's job performance (past or present), this can be taken into consideration in decisions of hiring and promotion. It can therefore be interpreted that, in most instances, to be protected a person must not be currently afflicted with the condition (that is, in a way that interferes with performance). Likewise, students who use drugs or alcohol in violation of institutional rules may be disciplined without conflicting with Section 504.

Because Section 504 is, at its core, concerned with bettering the opportunities and experiences of handicapped persons, many of whom are students, it is the particular role of student affairs administrators to assume leadership in coordinating their institution's compliance efforts. Since some of the areas covered under Section 504 are not exclusively within the purview of the typical student affairs division, this may necessitate cooperating with other campus employees (for example, faculty, admissions, conference planners) to ensure that all Section 504 mandates are understood and followed.

Employment. With regard to employment, Section 504 provides that "no qualified handicapped person shall, on the basis of handicap, be subjected to discrimination in employment" (34 C.F.R. § 104.11 [a] [1]). In this context, the term employment is very broad and includes a laundry list of activities, from recruitment and applications to promotion and termination (see 34 C.F.R. § 104.11 [b]). Furthermore, institutions are required to make "reasonable accommodation" to the known limitations of an otherwise qualified handicapped person unless it can show that the accommodation would impose an undue hardship on the institution. Reasonable accommodation may include making facilities accessible and usable, restructuring jobs, modifying equipment, and other similar actions. A discussion of the terms "otherwise qualified" and "undue hardship" is a prerequisite to a fuller understanding of the act's employment requirements.

A handicapped person is considered otherwise qualified for employment if he or she can perform, with reasonable accommodation, the "essential functions" of the job in question. *Essential functions* connotes the intent by Congress that handicapped persons should not be precluded simply because they may have difficulty with tasks that are only marginally related to the job. Under this construction, an institution might have to realign job assignments between employees, relocate offices or jobs to facilities that are accessible and usable, or physically modify existing offices so that they accommodate a person's handicap. None of these actions, however, are required where an institution can demonstrate that the accommodation would impose an "undue hardship" upon them. Primary factors to be considered in determining undue hardship include the nature and cost of the accommodation needed and the size of the recipient's budget. This provision was the recognition by Congress that requiring all accommodations would be financially devastating to many recipients, particularly those with limited resources.

Facilities. Section 504 prohibits institutions from excluding handicapped persons from their programs or activities because their facilities are inaccessible or unusable. It requires institutions to operate their programs and activities so that they are, when viewed in their entirety, accessible to handicapped persons. It is important to note that this does not require structural changes so that all existing facilities are made accessible, so long as programs on the whole are accessible. In its analysis of this provision, the DE specifically pointed out that "a university does not have to make all of its existing classroom buildings accessible to handicapped students if some of its buildings are already accessible and if it is possible to reschedule or relocate enough classes so as to offer all required courses and a reasonable selection of elective courses in accessible facilities" (34 C.F.R. § 104 Appendix A, Subpart C [20]). Thus, structural changes to existing facilities are only required when there are no other means of making an institution's programs accessible.

In regard to the construction of new facilities or the alteration of existing ones, Section 504 mandates that such construction be done in a way that ensures accessibility and usability by handicapped persons. In accomplishing this, institutions are required to follow the standards established by the American National Standards Institute Inc. in a document titled *American National Standard Specifications for Making Buildings and Facilities Accessible to, and Usable by, the Physically Handicapped* (see 34 C.F.R. § 104.23 [c]). Departure from these standards is permitted only if other methods are shown to provide equivalent access.

In the area of student housing, Section 504 requires institutions to "provide comparable, convenient, and accessible housing to handicapped students at the same cost as to others" (34 C.F.R. § 104.45 [a]). The overall objective of this requirement is to make sure that handicapped students are provided with housing options in sufficient quantity and variety so that, on the whole, their range of choice in living arrangements is comparable to that of other students.

Admissions and Recruitment. In the area of admissions and recruitment Section 504 provides that "qualified handicapped persons may not, on the basis of handicap, be denied admission or be subjected to discrimination in admission or recruitment" (34 C.F.R. § 104.42 [a]). Under this provision an institution may neither set limits on the number or proportion of handicapped students that it admits nor utilize admission tests or criteria that have a disproportionate, adverse effect on handicapped persons, unless the tests or criteria are valid predictors of success in the program and alternate tests (that is, that have a less adverse effect) are not available. Similarly, if an admissions test is given to a person who is handicapped in his or her sensory, manual, or speaking skills, an institution must administer the test so that the results reflect the person's aptitude or achievement level rather than impaired sensory, manual, or speaking skills (that is, except where the test is designed to measure those skills). Finally, unless an institution is taking remedial or voluntary action to overcome the effects of past discrimination, it may not make preadmission inquiries about the existence of an applicant's handicap. Upon admission, however, an institution may inquire on a confidential basis about those handicaps that may require accommodation.

Academic Adjustments. Section 504 requires an institution to "make such modifications to its academic requirements as are necessary to ensure that such requirements do not discriminate or have the effect of discriminating . . . against a qualified handicapped applicant or student" (34 C.F.R. § 104.44 [a]). Although this provision requires institutions to make modifications in certain areas (for example, examination requirements parallel those for admissions tests discussed earlier), it does not obligate them to waive courses or other academic requirements that are shown to be essential to the particular program of study or degree that is sought. In its analysis of the act, the DE provided the example of allowing a student who is deaf to replace a required course in music appreciation with a course in art appreciation or music history (see 34 C.F.R. § 104 Appendix A, Subpart E [31]). In addition, institutions may not enforce rules that have the effect of limiting participation by handicapped students, such as a prohibition of tape recorders, braille writers, or guide dogs in campus buildings. Finally, institutions must ensure that handicapped students are not discriminated against because of a lack of necessary educational auxiliary aids, such as interpreters, readers, or taped texts.

Financial and Employment Assistance and Nonacademic Services. Section 504 provides that institutions may not, on the basis of handicap, provide less financial assistance to handicapped students than for nonhandicapped students, nor limit a handicapped student's eligibility for assistance on account of the handicap. Similarly, when providing assistance for obtaining outside employment for students, institutions must ensure that their services for handicapped students are, on the whole, comparable to those provided for nonhandicapped students (see 34 C.F.R. § 104.46 [a] and [b]).

In the area of nonacademic services, Section 504 requires institutions that offer physical education courses or intercollegiate, club, or intramural athletics to provide handicapped students "an equal opportunity for participation in these activities" (34 C.F.R. § 104.47 [a] [1]). Furthermore, institutions that offer counseling and placement services to their students must provide these in a nondiscriminatory fashion, particularly ensuring that "qualified handicapped students are not counseled toward more restrictive career objectives than are nonhandicapped students with similar interests and abilities" (34 C.F.R. § 104.47 [b]). Finally, institutions that provide assistance to fraternities, sororities, and other similar organizations must ensure that these organizations do not discriminate against handicapped persons in their membership practices or as otherwise prohibited under the act.

Although the preceding discussion of Section 504 provides only a general overview of the act's requirements, it should serve as a starting point for further exploration of institutional obligations under the act. To become more familiar with Section 504 and its mandates, administrators should obtain and read the act's implementing regulations (34 C.F.R. Part 104) as well as key judicial decisions that have interpreted the act (particularly *Southeastern Community College v. Davis* [1979] and *School Board of Nassau County Florida v. Arline* [1987]). Finally, competent legal counsel should be consulted whenever a campus decision may have implications under Section 504.

Complaints. The responsibility of enforcing Section 504 is divided between the DE and the individual institutions under its purview. With an appointed employee responsible for administering compliance at each institution, the college or university serves as the first line of compliance by investigating any allegations of discrimination and administering grievance procedures. The regulations make clear that exhaustion of institutional procedures is not necessary for the DE to take its own action, but it is highly encouraged. In addition, although the statute itself is unclear about whether a private right of action exists, case law has held that such a right exists. (See *Lloyd v. Regional Transp. Auth.*, 1977.)

Once the DE has made a determination that discrimination has occurred, an institution is required to take remedial action (that is, at the direction of the DE) or face the ultimate penalty of losing all federal funding. Possible actions can include the provision of services to people previously discriminated against, the creation of a remedial action plan, the reinstatement of former employees, or any combination of these as well as additional steps to address the effects of past or current discrimination. Under any circumstances, the potential cost to the institution, both in monetary and reputational terms (that is, potential attorney fees, physical restructuring, hours of labor for staff), can be substantial and highly unpredictable. This emphasizes each institution's need to be completely aware of its obligations under Section 504, so that it may take preventative measures to ensure compliance, protect limited funds from allegations of discrimination, and most importantly, promote an environment that is accessible to and supportive of handicapped persons. On this note, each affected institution would be well advised to conduct periodical reviews (that is, every one to three years) of its compliance efforts and take voluntary action where necessary.

The Americans with Disabilities Act

Passed by the U.S. Congress in 1990, the Americans with Disabilities Act (ADA) (see Appendix) was enacted to expand protection for individuals with disabilities in the various areas of employment, public services, public accommodations, and telecommunications services (note that the ADA uses the term *disability* as opposed to *handicap* under Section 504).

Coverage. Although its mandates are very similar to Section 504's, the ADA applies not only to recipients of federal financial assistance but also to purely private sector entities. Because of the act's relative newness and a corresponding lack of judicial decisions interpreting it, attention should be given to analogous provisions under Section 504 for an understanding of how the ADA will apply. As far as its impact on institutions of higher education is concerned, its primary effects will be in the areas of employment, academic programs, and facility construction. Because those provisions respecting academic programs and facility construction closely match those of Section 504, readers should look to Section 504 case law (and the previous discussion in this chapter) for an analysis of how ADA will affect academic programs and facility construction (see 42 U.S.C. § 12183). The following discussion will address the ADA's impact on employment.

The ADA provides that "no covered entity shall discriminate against a qualified individual with a disability because of the disability of such individual in regard to job application procedures, the hiring, advancement, or discharge of employees, employee compensation, job training, and other terms, conditions, and privileges of employment" (42 U.S.C. § 12112 [a]). Covered entities include private and public (that is, government) employers as well as labor organizations and employment agencies but exclude Native American tribes and bona fide private membership clubs. Congress's use of the catchall phrase "other terms, conditions, and privileges of employment" clearly indicates its intent that the ADA, like Section 504, apply to all aspects of the employee-employer relationship.

The ADA protects any "qualified individual with a disability," defined as "an individual with a disability who, with or without reasonable accommodation, can perform the essential functions of the employment position that such individual holds or desires" (42 U.S.C. § 12111 [8]) (Note that "reasonable accommodation" is defined similarly under the ADA as under Section 504.) The act uses a definition of "essential functions" that is analogous to that in Section 504, but it specifically points out that written job descriptions provided by an employer are evidence of the job's essential functions. Thus, administrators must define the essential qualifications in their position descriptions if this was not already done. In regard to specific disabilities covered, the ADA uses parallel language to Section 504 (that is, it defines disability as a physical or mental impairment that substantially limits one or more major life activities) but specifically excludes from the definition of disability "homosexuality, bisexuality, . . . transvestism, transsexualism, pedophilia, exhibitionism, voyeurism, gender identity disorders not resulting from physical impairments, . . . compulsive gambling, kleptomania, [and] pyromania" (42 U.S.C. § 12211 [a] and [b]). In addition, although rehabilitated drug addicts are covered under the ADA, current users of illegal drugs are not (similar to Section 504).

Although the ADA prohibits direct forms of discrimination in employment in much the same terms as Section 504, as pointed out by Friedman and Strickler (1993) it also expressly codifies a disproportionate impact theory of discrimination. For example, it forbids employers from "utilizing standards, criteria, or methods of administration . . . that have the effect of discrimination on the basis of disability" as well as "using qualification standards, employment tests or other selection criteria that screen out or tend to screen out" individuals or groups of individuals with disabilities (42 U.S.C. § 12112 [b] [3] and [6]). In so doing, "it is clear that Congress chose to explicate in some detail the manner by which an ADA plaintiff can establish a prima facie claim" of illegal discrimination (Friedman and Strickler, 1993, p. 963).

The defenses that an employer can assert to an alleged violation of the ADA are similar to those available under Section 504. Thus, it can show that its employment criteria that screen out or tend to screen out individuals with disabilities are "job related for the position in question and . . . consistent with business necessity" (42 U.S.C. § 12112 [b] [6]). Also, it can defend its decision not to make "reasonable accommodation" to the known disability of an individual (an affirmative duty under the ADA as under Section 504) by demonstrating "that the accommodation would impose an undue hardship on the operation of the business" (42 U.S.C. § 12112 [b] [5] [A]). The terms "reasonable accommodation" and "undue hardship" are defined similarly under the ADA as in Section 504, and their meaning must be determined on a case-by-case basis (although nonexclusive factors are provided under the ADA at 42 U.S.C. § 12111 [9] and [10], respectively). Finally, the ADA specifically points out that its standards are not to be construed as applying a lesser standard upon employers than those of Section 504 (see 42 U.S.C. § 12201 [a]).

Complaints. The EEOC, Office of the Attorney General, and Office of Federal Contract Compliance Programs have primary enforcement responsibilities under the ADA (see 42 U.S.C. § 12117)). It should be noted that at least one case has held that exhaustion of administrative remedies is not necessary before a private action can be initiated (*Petersen v. U. of Wisconsin Bd. of Regents,* 1993). Furthermore, the act allows injured persons to recover both compensatory and punitive damages for discriminatory behavior, and it also prohibits coercion, retaliation, or intimidation against anyone alleging discrimination against a covered entity (see 42 U.S.C. §12203). Finally, the act requires employers to "post notices in an accessible format to applicants, employees, and members describing the applicable provisions" of the ADA upon their organization (42 U.S.C. § 12115).

Conclusion

The period from the mid-1950s to the early 1970s is commonly referred to as the civil rights era, and occasionally as the second reconstruction (Belton, 1992). The beginning of this era is usually marked by the landmark Supreme Court decision *Brown v. Board of Education* (1954), which ruled that segregated school systems were inherently unequal and therefore, in violation of the Fourteenth Amendment. All but one of the statutes introduced in this chapter were enacted during that period of time. However, debate about and legal challenges to these statutes have been numerous and will continue well into the future as this country grapples with the current effects of past discrimination, the scope and coverage of present statutes, continuing discrimination, and the appropriate federal role in civil rights.

The civil rights requirements placed on recipients of federal financial assistance represent "a major focus of federal spending policy, importing substantial social goals into education policy and making equality of educational opportunity a clear national priority" (Kaplin, 1985, p. 517). The role of the federal government "in the implementation and enforcement of civil rights [has] often been steeped in controversy . . . . [However] despite the controversy, it is clear that these federal civil rights efforts, over time, have provided a major force for social change in America" (Kaplin, 1985, p. 517).

References

Barr, M. J. "Sources of Laws Influencing Administrative Decisions in Student Affairs." In M. J. Barr (ed.), *Student Services and the Law.* San Francisco: Jossey-Bass, 1988.

Belton, R. "The Civil Rights Act of 1991 and the Future of Affirmative Action: A Preliminary Assessment." *DePaul Law Review,* 1992, *41,* 1085–1116.

Friedman, J. W., and Strickler, G. M. *Cases and Materials on the Law of Employment Discrimination.* (3rd ed.) Westbury, N.Y.: Foundation Press, 1993.

Gehring, D. G. "Legal Issues in the Administration of Student Affairs." In T. K. Miller and R. B. Winston, Jr. (eds.), *Administration and Leadership in Student Affairs: Actualizing Student Development in Higher Education.* (2nd ed.) Muncie, Ind.: Accelerated Development, 1991.

Haney, M. C. "Litigation of a Sexual Harassment Case After the Civil Rights Act of 1991." *Notre Dame Law Review,* 1993, *68,* 1037–1056.

Kaplin, W. A. *The Law of Higher Education: A Comprehensive Guide to Legal Implications of Administrative Decision Making.* (2nd ed., rev.) San Francisco: Jossey-Bass, 1985.

Player, M. A., Shoben, E. W., and Lieberwitz, R. L. *Employment Discrimination Law, Cases, and Materials.* St. Paul, Minn.: West, 1992.

Seaquist, G. "Civil Rights and Equal Access: When Laws Apply—And When They Do Not." In M. J. Barr and Associates (eds.), *Student Services and the Law: A Handbook for Practitioners.* San Francisco: Jossey-Bass, 1988.

Cases

Brown v. Board of Education, 347 U.S. 483 (1954).

Burton v. Wilmington Parking Authority, 365 U.S. 715 (1961).

DeSantis v. Pacific Tel. and Tel. Co., 608 F.2d 327 (9th Cir. 1979).

General Electric Co. v. Gilbert, 429 U.S. 125 (1976).

Grove City v. Bell, 104 S. Ct. 1211 (1984).

Lloyd v. Regional Transp. Auth., 548 F.2d 1277 (7th Cir. 1977).

Meritor Savings Bank v. Vinson, 477 U.S. 57 (1986).

Petersen v. U. of Wisconsin Bd. of Regents, 818 F. Supp. 1276 (W.D. Wis. 1993).

Robinson v. Eastern Kentucky University, 475 F.2d 707 (6th Cir. 1973); cert. den 416 U.S. 982.

School Board of Nassau County Florida v. Arline, 480 U.S. 273 (1987).

Southeastern Community College v. Davis, 442 U.S. 397 (1979).

TIMOTHY A. BILLS is coordinator of residence halls at Arizona State University and is pursuing a Ph.D. in higher education administration at Bowling Green State University. He is a member of the Association for Student Judicial Affairs.

PATRICK J. HALL is coordinator of chapter services for Greek life at Bowling Green State University, where he is pursuing a Ph.D. in higher education administration. He is a member of the Ohio state bar, the American Bar Association, and the Association for Student Judicial Affairs.

Recent protective policy laws have created a new in loco parentis law requiring institutional administrators to inform adults of drug and alcohol laws, graduation rates, crime statistics, and their right to privacy.

Protective Policy Laws

Donald D. Gehring

The laws and regulations discussed in Chapter Three all reflected the federal government's redistributive policy. They were also all enacted before the end of 1974 (that is, Title VI, Title VII, Title IX, Section 504, and the Vietnam Veterans' Readjustment Act), except for two of them—the Americans with Disabilities Act (ADA) and Age Discrimination in Education—and are generally modeled after laws passed before 1974. It was in that year that the emphasis of the government's regulation of higher education shifted from redistributive to protective policy. As noted in Chapter Two, protective policies are designed to intervene in private activities by setting conditions under which those activities may be conducted. The government therefore determines what is harmful and prohibits it while requiring conditions that are beneficial. Thus, because it has an impact on their work, those charged with responsibility for the out-of-class life (the private conduct) of students must be familiar with the changing federal climate. The purpose of this chapter is to assist student affairs administrators understand protective policy laws and regulations and how they affect campus policies, practices, and procedures.

The protective policy laws discussed in this chapter include the Family Educational Rights and Privacy Act (FERPA), more popularly known as the Buckley Amendment, after its author Senator James L. Buckley; the Student Consumer Information Act and its amendments, the Student Right-to-Know and Campus Security Act, and the Sexual Assault Victims' Bill of Rights; and the Drug Free Schools and Communities Act and its 1989 amendments. These laws apply to every institution that receives federal financial assistance or has students in attendance who receive funds under Title IV of the Higher Education Act of 1965 (including Pell Grants, Trio Programs, Stafford, PLUS, and Federal Perkins loans as well as federal work-study programs). Failing to comply with any of these laws and regulations can result in the termination or withholding of federal financial assistance. In addition, an institution that fails to comply with the Drug Free Schools and Communities Act as amended may also be required to repay "any or all forms of federal financial assistance received . . . when it was in violation . . . ." (34 C.F.R. § 86.301 [b] [1]).

The Buckley Amendment

On August 21, 1974, Gerald Ford, who had recently been elevated from his position of vice president to president after the resignation of Richard Nixon, signed into law his first piece of legislation, the Educational Amendments of 1974. This law amended and extended the Elementary and Secondary Education Act of 1965. Without the benefit of committee hearings, Senator James L. Buckley added an amendment to the bill titled "Protection of the Rights and Privacy of Parents and Students." This law is now known by its popular title—the Buckley Amendment—although its official title is the Family Educational Rights and Privacy Act (FERPA).

The Buckley Amendment is probably one of the most misunderstood pieces of legislation. Not having had the benefit of committee hearings, as first written it prohibited, for example, the publication of all personally identifiable information—even such information as the height, weight, or home town of athletes. Thus, on December 31, 1974, not long after FERPA became law, it was already amended to correct "inconsistent references to 'personally identifiable information, school records,' etc." (1974 U.S. Code Cong. and Admin. News 6794). Among other changes, the December 31, 1974, amendment substituted the generic words "the educational records of their children" for a laundry list of data that were to be available to parents and students. The amendment also defined "educational records" as "those records, files, documents and other materials that (i) contain information directly related to a student; and (ii) are maintained by the educational agency or institution or by a person acting for such agency or institution" (20 U.S.C.S. § 1232 G). The definition also included items that were not considered to be "educational records." Private letters of recommendation not maintained by the institution have been held not to be educational records under FERPA (*Olsson v. Indiana Univ. Bd. of Trustees*, 1991).

Unlike the redistributive laws described in Chapter Three, which generally state that no person of a protected class (for example, based on race or sex) can be excluded from or denied the benefits of any educational program or activity receiving federal funding, FERPA states that "no funds shall be made available under any applicable program to any . . . institution which has a policy of denying . . . the parents of students . . . the right to inspect and review the educational records of their children." The Buckley Amendment also states that "no funds shall be made available . . . to any . . . institution which has a policy or practice of permitting the release of educational records . . . of students without the written consent of their parents (20 U.S.C.S. § 1232 g). Thus, the intent of the redistributive laws are clearly spelled out—

they prohibit the denial of benefits to certain protected individuals. In contrast, Buckley does not prohibit anything. It simply states that funds will not be made available to institutions that have certain policies and practices.

Even the executive and judicial branches of government cannot agree on the intent of the Buckley Amendment. For example, the secretary of education has issued regulations to implement the Buckley Amendment (see Appendix) that state, "The purpose of this part is to set out requirements for the protection of privacy of parents and students under section 438 of the General Education Provisions Act as amended" (34 C.F.R. § 99.2). In contrast, both state and federal courts have said that "the underlying purpose of FERPA was not to grant individual students a right to privacy or access to educational records, but to stem the growing policy of many institutions to carelessly release educational information" (*Bauer v. Kincaid*, 1991, p. 590. Also see *Smith v. Duquesne University*, 1985; *Student Bar Ass'n. Bd. of Governors, Etc. v. Byrd*, 1977; *Red and Black Pub. Co., Inc. v. Board of Regents*, 1993). However, confusion exists even within the judiciary with one court stating that "the intent of Congress to withhold millions of federal dollars from universities that violate Buckley is ample prohibition, regardless of how the word 'prohibit' is construed " (*The Shreveport Professional Chapter of the Society of Professional Journalists and Michelle Millhollon v. Louisiana State University in Shreveport*, 1994).

Individuals have requested access under state freedom of information laws to campus crime reports (*Bauer v. Kincaid*, 1991), student organization court proceedings (*Red and Black Pub. Co., Inc. v. Board of Regents*, 1993), and faculty meetings where individual students were to be discussed (*Student Bar Ass'n. Bd. of Governors, Etc. v. Byrd*, 1977). Institutions have attempted to fend off these requests by pointing out that their state freedom of information acts exempt "records protected from disclosure by law" and that the Buckley Amendment protects from disclosure the information that is sought. The courts, however, have permitted access because FERPA is *not a law prohibiting the disclosure of records;* it only denies funds to institutions that have a policy or practice of disclosing personally identifiable information without a student's consent.

Most states have freedom of information acts (FOIA), which guarantee citizens access to government decision making and records (private institutions are not governed by FOIAs). Many states also have laws directly prohibiting the release of certain student records (for example, Arizona, A.R.S. § 15–151 et seq.). As the previous discussion demonstrated, both of these types of state laws intersect with FERPA (see for example *Kestenbaum v. Michigan State University*, 1982). Thus student affairs administrators must be familiar with their state FOIAs and student record statutes as well as with the Buckley Amendment.

Another troublesome aspect of FERPA for many administrators is that it is a permissive law. FERPA permits the institution to make certain important decisions. For example, the institution may decide what constitutes directory information (information that can be disclosed without the student's consent) within the general parameters of information "not generally considered harmful or an invasion of privacy if disclosed" (34 C.F.R. § 99.3). However, institutions are not required by FERPA to categorize any data as directory information and cannot be compelled under FERPA to disclose even students' names and addresses if those items are not defined by the institution as directory information (*Krauss v. Nassau Community College*, 1983). Institutions may also decide which persons are "school officials" and what constitutes a "legitimate educational interest" in their determination of who may access educational records without a student's consent. The law permits but does not require institutions to allow parents of financially dependent students to access their son or daughter's records without the child's consent. The institution must, however, by law, have a written policy that spells out these discretionary decisions and several other items and that must be available upon request (34 C.F.R. § 99.6). Students must be informed annually about how and where to obtain a copy of this policy, given a statement of their rights under FERPA, and told how to initiate a complaint (34 C.F.R. § 99.7). The rules offer a great deal of latitude in providing this annual notification. It may be done "by any means that are reasonably likely to inform . . . students of their rights" (34 C.F.R. § 9.7[C]).

Once an individual is in attendance at a postsecondary institution, no matter his or her age, the rights granted under FERPA become those of the student rather than of the parent (34 C.F.R. § 99.5). This is especially significant for institutions where students under the age of 18 regularly enroll. In Ohio, for example, high school juniors and seniors may attend college on a full-time basis under a state mandated program (R.C. 3365.01 et seq.). Institutions throughout the country operate Trio and other independent programs where minors are regularly brought to the campus and actually enroll in classes and live in residence halls. Student affairs administrators should review their FERPA policy to ensure that the statements providing or denying parents access to student records clearly articulate what is desired with respect to minor students. A FERPA policy may differentiate between dependent students who are under 18 years of age and adult dependent students. (It should be remembered that FERPA permits institutions to decide whether to allow parents of dependent students access to student's records without the student's consent.) Public institutions that can show a rational relationship between the legitimate interests of the state and the differential treatment would not run counter to the equal protection clause of the Fourteenth Amendment (see *Stone v. Cornell University*, 1987).

FERPA's definition of a student, however, is somewhat tricky. The rules (see Appendix) state that a student is any individual "who is or has been in attendance at . . . an institution and regarding whom the . . . institution maintains educational records" (34 C.F.R. § 99.3). This definition obviously includes former students. Thus former students have the right to review and inspect their records, and the institution may not release those records without complying with FERPA. The definition of the word *student* in the regulations and the legislative history of the act also make it clear that an individual who has been denied admission is not a student and therefore has no rights under FERPA (120 Cong. Rec. 39,863, 1974). For example, a student attending the College of Arts and Sciences at X University who is denied admission to the Graduate School of X University (or to any other college or unit within X University) would not have FERPA rights to the admissions file maintained by the graduate school. Obviously, the student would have FERPA rights to the educational records regarding his or her status as an A & S student in the institution. Individuals who are denied regular admission but who audit classes would have FERPA rights regarding the class they audit but not regarding the admission file (*Tarka v. Franklin,* 1989).

A student's right to inspect his or her records does not mean the student has a right to a copy of the records. Only if denying the student a copy would effectively prevent the student from inspecting the record is it necessary to provide a copy (34 C.F.R. § 99.1 [d]). This situation might arise if a former student living some distance from the campus wanted to inspect or review a record. The institution may charge a fee for providing copies but not for searching for or retrieving the record (34 C.F.R. § 99.11). Institutions may also require that all outstanding charges be paid before an official transcript is issued without being in conflict with FERPA (*Spas v. Wharton,* 1980). Although students have the right to inspect their records they may not use FERPA as "a means by which [to] . . . obtain information on how a particular grade was assigned. At most, a student is only entitled to know whether or not the assigned grade was recorded accurately in the student's record" (*Tarka v. Cunningham,* 1990, p. 1282).

There are many exceptions to students' rights to inspect their records. They do not have a right under FERPA to inspect or review the financial records of their parents or the records of other students that may be contained in their educational records; the private notes of officials that are not shared with others; or medical and psychological records. However, students do have a right to have qualified individuals review their medical and psychological records and provide an interpretation to them.

Some colleges and universities continue the practice of posting students' grades, using a class roster listing ID numbers but deleting individual names. This practice violates the disclosure-without-consent section of FERPA because class rosters are printed in alphabetical order. In one court's estimation this allows grades to be correlated with individual names even when the roster contains the scores of seventy-five individuals (*Kryston v. Board of Ed. East Ramapo, Etc.,* 1980). Thus, since the grades can be personally identifiable, they may not be disclosed in this manner without the written consent of the students.

There are many exceptions to FERPA's indirect prohibition against disclosure without consent. As stated earlier, information from students' educational records may be disclosed to the parents of financially dependent students (defined to mean students whom the parents claim as tax deductions) without their consent. Information from a student's record may also be disclosed in an emergency situation if that information "is necessary to protect the health or safety of the student or other individuals" (34 C.F.R. § 99.36). The disclosure of information to "other school officials" who have "legitimate educational interests" in the information and the disclosure of data in connection with a student's application for financial aid do not require the student's consent. Administrators may also disclose information without the student's consent in response to lawfully issued subpoenas, but they must first make reasonable efforts to notify the student of the subpoena (*State v. Birdsall,* 1977). Other exceptions to the disclosure-without-consent section exist in the regulations, and administrators should familiarize themselves with them.

The Student Right-to-Know and Campus Security Act (see Appendix) also amended FERPA, providing yet another exception to the disclosure-without-consent section. This amendment allows but does not require institutions to disclose to the alleged victim of a violent crime the results of any disciplinary proceeding against the alleged perpetrator of the crime. Crimes of violence are generally defined as a felony (administrators will now need to know what constitutes a felony) or an offense in which there is the attempted, threatened, or actual use of force (18 U.S.C. § 16). However, the Sexual Assault Victims' Bill of Rights (see Appendix) specifies that for campus disciplinary proceedings involving sexual assaults both the accuser and accused shall be informed of the outcome (20 U.S.C. § 1092 [7] [B] [iv]). Thus, while institutions may or may not inform the alleged victim of a crime of violence about the outcome of the disciplinary proceeding, they *must* inform both the accuser and the accused of the outcome when it is a matter of sexual assault. There is a problem here, however. If the particular sexual offense is not a crime of violence (it is not a felony and does not involve attempted, threatened, or actual use of physical force), FERPA does not permit disclosure of the outcome of the disciplinary proceeding without the written consent of the accused because the proceedings become a personally identifiable record maintained by the institution about that student. Efforts to obtain an interpretation on this point from various federal offices have proven fruitless. Student affairs administrators should consult with counsel before informing the accuser of the results of disciplinary proceedings against the accused when there has been a sexual offense that was not a crime of violence as defined by 18 U.S.C. § 16. Finally, at the time of this writing, the secretary of education has issued proposed rules implying that campus disciplinary actions or proceedings are educational records and thus require a student's consent before being disclosed.

The regulations also provide several exceptions to the inspect-and-review requirements. The most notable exception is that institutions need not permit students access to financial records (34 C.F.R. § 99.12). Other exceptions are created by excluding certain information from the definition of educational records. For example, a hall director who maintains anecdotal notes on students in the hall but does not share them with anyone else, except a short-term substitute filling in while the hall director attends a conference, need not give students access to those notes. Therefore, students do not have a right to inspect such notes (34 C.F.R. § 99.3). Recently (on July 23, 1993), Congress amended FERPA also to exclude from the definition of educational records those records created and maintained by campus law enforcement personnel for the purpose of law enforcement (P.L. 102–325, Title XV, Part H, § 1555 [a]). Because these campus police records are no longer considered educational records, they may be disclosed without the student's consent. Current proposed rules concerning records relating to disciplinary proceedings by the institution specifically state that such records are not law enforcement records, even if they come into possession of the law enforcement unit, so long as they are not maintained by the law enforcement unit. Thus, if the proposed rules remain intact, students would have a right to inspect their disciplinary records and institutions would not be able to disclose them (except in the case of crimes of violence) without the student's consent.

Students have the right under FERPA to challenge, in a formal hearing at which they may be represented by counsel, information in their educational records that is inaccurate, misleading, or in violation of their right of privacy (34 C.F.R. § 9.20, 99.21, 99.22). Student affairs administrators should review these regulations to ensure that their procedures for hearings at which students could challenge information in their records are in conformance with the regulations. Administrators should also review the information maintained in various student files to determine whether all the information there is really necessary. Nothing in FERPA prohibits purging a file (unless there has been a request to inspect the file).

The Buckley Amendment does not provide a private right of action (*Price v. Young,* 1983; *Tarka v. Franklin,* 1989; *Klein Independent School District v. Mattox,* 1987). This means that a student may not initiate a civil suit to enforce FERPA rights. However, a suit can be brought for damages (financial losses) against public institutional administrators who can be shown to have violated an individual's rights under FERPA (*Fay v. South Colonie Cent. School Dist.,* 1986).

Several times in this section it has been suggested that administrators review their policies and practices and the FERPA regulations. The citation for the FERPA regulations is listed in Appendix, and most university libraries have copies of the Code of Federal Regulations. However, it is advisable to review the final regulations as they appear in the Federal Register, Vol. 53, No. 69, Apr. 11, 1988, at page 11942, because these regulations are followed by a text titled "Analysis of Comments and Changes." This analysis offers a better understanding of the thinking and rationale of the rule makers. If all else fails, student affairs administrators can call FERPA at (202) 732-1807 with any questions. These people are there to offer technical assistance and, further, are unusually pleasant people to deal with, by Washington standards.

Student Consumer Information

The Higher Education Act of 1965 (see Appendix) is the most comprehensive federal law concerning higher education. The law contains a variety of titles including Academic Library and Information Technology; Institutional Aid; Educator Recruitment, Retention and Development; International Education; Indian Higher Education; Community Service; Cooperative Education; Construction, Reconstruction, and Renovation of Academic Facilities; Graduate Programs and Postsecondary Improvement Programs, among others. Title IV of the act provides for numerous student assistance programs including a variety of grants, loans, and work-study programs. More than a decade after its passage (on October 12, 1976), a significant amendment was added to Title IV in the form of the Educational Amendments of 1976 (P.L. 94–482). They added a general provision to Title IV titled "Student Consumer Information," which requires institutions receiving funds under Title IV to disseminate a broad range of consumer information to current and prospective students. Congress, recognizing the size and complexity of student aid programs, also directed the commissioner of education (there was no separate cabinet-level department for education at the time; it was a unit within the Department of Health, Education, and Welfare) to survey institutional practices, convene meetings of financial aid administrators, explore means of disseminating financial aid information, and include peer counselors in training sessions. The amendment also provided incentive matching grants to states to increase the proficiency of state financial aid administrators.

There have been several amendments to the original "Student Consumer Information" section of Title IV, most notably the recently enacted Student Right-to-Know and Campus Security Act as amended by the originally titled Campus Sexual Assault Victims' Bill of Rights. The law with all of its amendments may be found in its entirety in the United States Code and is now known formally as "Institutional and Financial Assistance Information for Students" (see Appendix). However, regulations only exist at this writing for the older "Student Consumer Information Services" (see Appendix). Regulations to implement the student right-to-know portion of the act as amended have only been published as proposed rules at this writing (see 57 Fed. Reg. 30826, July 10, 1992). Final regulations to implement the campus security portion have, however, been published (see Appendix).

Institutions receiving student assistance funds under Title IV must, by law, make information readily available to all current (including part-time) students and to prospective students (those who contact the institution and request information concerning admission) who request it. Like the Buckley Amendment, the regulations provide institutions with a great deal of latitude in deciding how to promulgate the information. Institutions "shall disseminate [the information] . . . through appropriate publications and mailing" (34 C.F.R. § 668.41). Most institutions have developed a single financial aid brochure that contains much of the required information.

Generally, the information required to be disseminated is of two types: (1) information about the institution; and (2) information about the various types of student financial assistance available at the institution. The first type includes the following: (1) tuition and fees for full- and part-time students;

(2) estimates of the cost of books and supplies, room and board charges, and transportation costs; (3) any additional program costs; (4) refund policies; (5) current degree and training programs; (6) laboratory and other physical facilities relating to the academic program; and (7) the faculty and other instructional personnel.

Originally institutions were also required to provide retention data and the number and percentage of students completing programs; however, in 1980 the 96th Congress found that "such data is very costly and difficult to obtain and frequently misleading" (H.R. Rep. No. 96–520, 96th Cong., 2nd Sess. [1980] reprinted in 1980 U.S. Code Cong. and Admin. News 3183). About a decade later the 101st Congress, in passing the Student Right-to-Know and Campus Security Act, decided their predecessors were wrong and said that "knowledge of graduation rates would help prospective students and prospective student athletes make an informed judgment about the educational benefits available at a given institution of higher education" (P.L. 101–542, Sec. 102, Nov. 8, 1990). In a very persuasive argument, Astin (1993) disagreed with this statement and pointed out that reporting the graduation rates could actually be misleading—something the 96th Congress recognized.

The 96th Congress also included additional information about the institution that must now be disseminated, including information on facilities and services available to disabled students and organizations that have accredited the institution (P.L. 96–374).

The information about student financial assistance that must also be disseminated includes (1) a description of all financial assistance programs available, including those based on need and those that are not; (2) the eligibility requirements for assistance, forms and procedures to be completed to apply for assistance, and the criteria used to select recipients and determine the amount of the award; (3) the rights and responsibilities of students receiving aid; (4) criteria for continued eligibility, maintaining satisfactory progress (added by P.L. 96–374), and reestablishing eligibility; (5) how disbursements will be made; (6) the terms of any loans and a sample repayment schedule; and (7) conditions and terms of employment for work-study students.

Finally, the law requires that institutions provide exit counseling for students who have borrowed money under any one of the loan programs. This counseling should include a discussion of anticipated monthly repayments and repayment options as well as general information concerning the average indebtedness of students who have Stafford or Perkins loans. The counseling may be done individually or in groups, but if a student leaves the institution before such counseling the information must be provided in writing.

As already discussed, there have been several amendments to the student consumer information section of Title IV. Notice of the changes is usually sent to the financial aid officer. For both of these reasons, student affairs administrators should initiate discussions with the financial aid officer to determine whether the institution's data are in compliance with all current rules, in what way the information is made "readily available," in what way it is made available to prospective students who request it, and what the practices are with respect to exit counseling. Institutions that fail to comply with the requirements could become embroiled in a breach of contract suit resulting in an order to repay tuition and fees (*James v. SCS Business and Technical Inst.,* 1992).

An interesting aspect of the requirements of the student consumer information section is the necessity to provide students with information concerning "the institution's faculty and *other instructional personnel*" [emphasis added, 34 C.F.R. § 668.44 (a) (4) (iii)]. Most institutions that use graduate students to teach classes or conduct labs seldom if ever make that fact known in their publications. Student affairs administrators may want to discuss this with the academic personnel at the institution.

Student Right-to-Know

The student consumer information section of Title IV was recently amended by the Student Right-to-Know and Campus Security Act as amended by the Sexual Assault Victims' Bill of Rights (see Appendix 1). The laws were enacted "to provide students and parents with better information in selecting a post-secondary institution" (H.R. Rep. 101–518, 101st Cong., 2nd Sess. [1990] reprinted in 1990 U.S. Code Cong. and Admin. News 3364), but as noted earlier, Astin (1993) argued that, at least with respect to the data required by the student right-to-know section, the law may have just the opposite result and, in fact, be misleading. The campus security section also has the potential to be misleading. On many campuses crimes are never reported (Palmer, 1993) and therefore they would never appear in the data required under the campus security section of the law.

As noted earlier, the student right-to-know section reintroduced the requirement to compile graduation rate data. The reporting of these data generally follows the requirements of the student consumer information law that it amends by mandating that graduation rate data for students, as a whole, be "readily available." However, institutions now are required, in addition, to provide graduation rate data of athletes on financial aid categorized by race, sex, and sport and *must provide that data to each prospective athlete to whom an offer is made.*

The law specifies that graduation rate data be computed by using cohorts entering the institution between July 1 and September 30 as full-time degree-seeking undergraduates who are first-time attendees at any postsecondary institution. Thus, students who transfer into the institution are excluded as are those who transfer out to an advanced program for which their prior program was a substantial preparation. Also excluded are those who enter the military, government foreign service, or the church. Because of the exclusion from the cohort of transfer students and others, institutions will probably need to begin collecting data that they did not collect before. The method of data collection will also change. To ensure accurate graduation rate data, exit interviews will become imperative to determine why an individual left the institution. It is interesting that there is an exemption from the cohort for "church service" while individuals who are atheists or do not belong to a church are included in the cohort. This exemption may be challenged as a violation of the First Amendment clause prohibiting the establishment of religion either under the primary purpose or excessive entanglement prongs of *Lemon v. Kurtzman* (1971).

Graduation rates are calculated using 150 percent of the normal program length (that is, six years for a normal bachelor's degree and three years for the typical associate's degree). Institutions may, however, provide supplemental data to illuminate graduation rate data. The data required under Student Right-to-Know must now be available covering the period from July 1, 1991 to June 30, 1992; however, where institutions have not maintained graduation rate data they may use the persistence rate of the cohort that entered in fall 1991 until graduation rate data are available. The government expects that graduation rate data will be available at every institution for the 1991 cohort no later than July 1, 1998.

Regulations to implement this section of the law have not been published at this writing. When they are published they will be sent to the financial aid officer. Because this law involves so many campus offices—financial aid, admissions, athletics, and registration—it is suggested that a task force or committee be established to ensure that all necessary data are collected accurately.

Campus Security

A variety of campus offices will also need to collaborate in compiling the data required by the campus security section as amended. Generally, the law requires institutions to maintain and annually distribute "through appropriate publications and mailings to all current students *and employees* and to any applicant for enrollment or employment upon request" (P.L. 101–542, Sec. 204[f]) campus crime statistics, various policy statements, and sexual assault programs. The policies affect, at the least, campus law enforcement, housing, Greek life, physical plant, counseling, judicial affairs, health services, academic affairs, and personnel.

Crime statistics must be complied annually on a calendar-year basis for all *reported* murders, robberies (the definition requires the use or threat of force or violence in the taking of another's property), aggravated assaults (generally an intention to do physical harm in the commission of a crime), auto thefts, burglaries (generally requires breaking and entering with intent to commit a felony), and sexual offenses. Forcible acts are included. ("Any sexual act directed against another person, forcibly and/or (sic) against that person's will; or not forcibly or against the person's will where the victim is incapable of giving consent." This includes forcible rape, forcible sodomy, sexual assault with an object, and forcible fondling [U.S. Department of Justice, 1992, pp. 21–22].) Nonforcible acts are also included. ("Unlawful, nonforcible sexual intercourse." This includes incest and statutory rape [U.S. Department of

Justice, 1992, p. 22].) Statistics must also be kept on *arrests* for weapons, drug abuse, and alcohol violations occurring on campus, which includes private property owned or controlled by recognized student organizations.

By requiring that such information be kept, Congress is attempting to alert parents, students, and others to the fact that serious crimes do take place on college campuses. However, this reporting requirement will also provide confusing and misleading data to the public. The law requires that campus crimes only be reported because it would be difficult to include crimes outside the jurisdiction of campus law enforcement. However, for some colleges, notably urban institutions, where crime may be more prevalent on streets bordering the campus than on the campus itself, the institution may appear relatively safe when in fact it isn't. Also, the statistics may be an indication of how free students, faculty, and staff feel to report crime or how vigorously campus police enforce the law rather than an indication of the safety of the campus.

The policies that are required to be documented and distributed include (1) crime reporting procedures and facilities and the institution's response to reports of criminal activity; (2) the security of facilities and access thereto; (3) campus police enforcement authority and relationships with external law enforcement agencies; (4) programs to inform the campus community about security procedures and practices; (5) monitoring and recording of criminal activity at off-campus student organizations; and (6) enforcement of underage drinking and drug laws.

The law also requires that timely reports be made to the campus community of all murders, robberies, aggravated assaults, auto thefts, and sexual offenses, both forcible and nonforcible, reported to either campus or local law enforcement agencies *that are considered to be a threat to other students and employees.* Administrators may want to establish specific places on campus where this type of information can be displayed without being lost in the myriad notices and announcements posted in campus buildings. This requirement is somewhat troublesome at this time because the rules to implement it define a campus law enforcement staff member as "an official of an institution who has significant responsibility for student and campus activities but does not have significant counseling responsibilities" (59 Fed. Reg. 22320, Apr. 29, 1994). Efforts by individuals and professional associations to exclude hall directors from the definition—thereby excluding them from the requirement to report crimes such as sexual offenses that they become aware of in their counseling of students—may have resulted in this broader definition. Housing officers and others may want to revise their position descriptions for some staff to include counseling as a significant responsibility.

The Campus Sexual Assault Victims' Bill of Rights adds to the information to be made available under the campus security section of the law. Additional information must include a description of (1) sexual assault and sexual offense awareness programs; (2) possible sanctions for sexual offenses; (3) procedures for students to follow once an offense has occurred; and (4) campus disciplinary procedures including the right in sexual assault cases to have others present during the proceedings and to be notified of the outcome (see earlier comments). Institutions must also notify students of (1) their option to report a sexual offense to external law enforcement units and to be assisted by campus administrators in doing so; (2) counseling and other victim services both on and off campus; and (3) their option to change living and academic arrangements where reasonably available and to be assisted by administrators in doing so. The secretary of education has interpreted this last requirement very broadly to include releasing a victim "from an on-campus housing contract without penalty . . . and assist[ing] the student to [locate] off-campus housing if it is reasonably available" (Summary of Proposed Changes, Student Assistance General Provisions, 58 Fed. Reg. 54904 [1993]). Furthermore, the final rules state that an institution's notice to students must specify that it "will change a victim's academic and living situations after an alleged sex offense . . . if those change are requested by the victim and are reasonably available" (59 Fed. Reg. 22319, Apr. 29, 1994. To be codified at 34 C.F.R. 668.47[a] [12]). Academic administrators will need to be aware of this requirement and options available for changing victims' academic situations. Where no other section of a course is available, completing the course on an independent study basis may be a reasonable alternative. Faculty generally do not enjoy it when others tell them how to conduct their classes, but in this situation administrators might prefer facing an antagonistic and disgruntled faculty member than losing all Title IV student aid funds.

Drug Free Schools and Communities Act and Amendments of 1989

Title XII of the Higher Education Act of 1965 required that institutions receiving funds under the act file a certificate with the secretary of education that the institution had a drug and alcohol abuse prevention program. On December 12, 1989, President Bush signed into law the Drug Free Schools and Communities Act Amendments (DFSCAA), setting out minimum standards for campus drug and alcohol abuse programs (see Appendix). Two essential requirements are mandated by DFSCAA—an annual written notice of five separate categories of information to students *and employees* and a biennial review of the effectiveness and consistency of the program.

The Drug Free Schools and Community Act Amendments differ from the previously discussed protective policy laws in two significant ways. While the Buckley Amendment and the Student Consumer Information acts essentially state that no funds will be made available to institutions that do not conform to the requirements of the respective laws, the DFSCAA states that if the secretary of education determines an institution is not in compliance with the law then, in addition, the institution may be required to repay all federal funds received during the period it was not in compliance. Although this is only one of several options open to the secretary, it represents a significant shift in policy. The other major difference is that under Buckley and Student Consumer Information the mandated notices and data must be disseminated either through "means that are likely to inform students of their rights" or "appropriate publications and mailings," respectively. Under DFSCAA, while the law did not specify that the notice must be in writing, the secretary determined (see regulations, Appendix) that "in order to ensure that each student has access to and can refer to the required materials they must be in writing" (Appendix C—Analysis of Comments and Responses, 55 Fed. Reg. 33595 [1990]). A study by Palmer, Gehring, and Guthrie (1992), however, indicated that written materials provided to students in compliance with the mandates of the regulations are one of the least effective means of transmitting the information required under DFSCAA. It is also one of the most inefficient means of disseminating the information since it is very expensive (Geraci, Guthrie, Key, and Parrott, 1990). Besides requiring that the notice be in writing, the regulations do not mandate how institutions are to distribute it to each student and employee. However, "merely making the materials available to those who wish to take them does not satisfy the requirements . . . because it does not ensure distribution to each student and employee" (Appendix C—Analysis of Comments and Responses, 55 Fed. Reg. 33595 [1990]). In this day of electronic and mail registration, it is difficult to ensure distribution without mailing copies of the notice.

The information required to be contained in the notice includes the following: (1) standards of conduct prohibiting, at a minimum, the unlawful use, possession, or distribution of illicit drugs and alcohol by students and employees; (2) a description of applicable laws related to unlawful possession or distribution of illicit drugs and alcohol; (3) a description of counseling and treatment programs available; (4) a clear statement that the institution will impose sanctions for violations of its standards and a description of those sanctions. This information must be distributed each year to each student and employee. Thus, if the notice is provided to students and employees in the fall term, each new student who enrolls in a subsequent term and each new employee appointed after the initial distribution must be provided a copy of the notice.

Students are defined only as those individuals enrolled for at least one "class" for academic credit (Appendix C—Analysis of Comments and Responses, 55 Fed. Reg. 33595 [1990]). Thus, individuals enrolled for CEU credits, auditors, and continuing education students need not receive the notice. Nor are institutions mandated to impose sanctions against them for unlawful use, possession, or distribution, although they may do so if they desire. However, the prohibition against unlawful use, possession, and distribution of illicit drugs and alcohol extends to students and employees at off-campus activities sponsored by the institution. Such activities include social and academic activities, including conferences where attendance is paid for by the institution.

The biennial review is required to be completed every two years with the first by late 1992 or early 1993. The review should be undertaken to determine the effectiveness of the program so that any necessary changes suggested by the review can be made. The second purpose of the review is to determine whether an institution's standards are consistently enforced and sanctions consistently applied. There is no standard format for the biennial review and each institution is free to design its own process; however, there must be a written report (more than anecdotal comments) that is available to the secretary and the public upon request. Institutions are not required to provide a copy of the report to anyone except as requested. Because the report is available to the public upon request, personally identifiable information should not be included. The report of the review must be kept for three years after the fiscal year in which it was created. Palmer (1992) provides a good discussion of how to conduct a biennial review.

Several references have been made here to the "Analysis of Comments and Responses." This analysis appears as an appendix to the final regulations published in the Federal Register and provides a much better understanding of the regulations and the Department of Education's interpretations than the basic regulations appearing in the Code of Federal Regulations (C.F.R.). An institution's librarian can procure a copy; it is a good idea for every administrator to obtain one and read it. The comments and responses appear with the regulations at 55 Fed. Reg. 33580 (1990). A copy also appears in *A Handbook for Complying with the Program and Review Requirements of the 1989 Amendments to the Drug Free Schools and Communities Act* (Palmer and Gehring, 1992).

Summary

In 1974 the federal government embarked on a course of protective policies in its relationship with higher education. This chapter was designed to assist administrators to understand better these protective laws and regulations and to provide an introduction to their requirements. One chapter, however, cannot provide the detail necessary to effectuate compliance. Only by reading the actual laws and regulations and in consultation with one's staff can one begin to develop a true understanding of how these laws affect one's institution's particular programs, policies, and practices. The laws and their regulations are not difficult to locate and the appendix is designed to aid that process. Campus libraries that are designated government document depositories should have copies of the Federal Register and the United States Code. Most county law libraries also have copies. It may be a good idea to appoint a member of the staff to research and provide copies of the laws and their regulations for all members and denote some staff development time to a discussion of how each law affects a particular area. The purpose of such discussions is to retain as much autonomy as possible for making educational decisions while complying with the law in a changing federal climate.

References

Astin, A. "College Retention Rates Are Often Misleading." *The Chronicle of Higher Education,* Sept. 22, 1993, p. A48.

Geraci, C., Guthrie, V., Key, R., and Parrott, D. "A Sampling of Responses by Higher Education to the 1989 Amendments to the Drug Free Schools and Communities Act, 1990." Unpublished manuscript, University of Louisville, Kentucky, 1990.

Palmer, C. J. "The Biennial Review." In C. J. Palmer and D. D. Gehring (eds.), *A Handbook for Complying with the Program and Review Requirements of the 1989 Amendments to the Drug-Free Schools and Communities Act.* Asheville, N.C.: College Administration Publications, 1992.

Palmer, C. J. *Violent Crimes and Other Forms of Victimization in Residence Halls.* Asheville, N.C.: College Administration Publications, 1993.

Palmer, C. J., and Gehring, D. D. (eds.). *A Handbook for Complying with the Program and Review Requirements of the 1989 Amendments to the Drug-free Schools and Communities Act.* Asheville, N.C.: College Administration Publications, 1992.

Palmer, C. J., Gehring, D. D., and Guthrie, V. L. "Student Knowledge of Information Mandated by the 1989 Amendments to the Drug Free Schools and Communities Act." *NASPA Journal,* 1992, *30,* 30–38.

U.S. Department of Justice. *Uniform Crime Reporting Handbook,* NIRBS Edition. Washington, D.C.: U.S. Department of Justice, 1992.

Cases

Bauer v. Kincaid, 759 F. Supp. 575 (W.D. Mo. 1991).

Fay v. South Colonie Cent. School Dist., 802 F., 2d 21 (2nd. Cir. 1986).

James v. SCS Business and Technical Inst., 595 N.Y.S. 2d 885 (Civ. Ct. N.Y. City 1992).

Kestenbaum v. Michigan State University, 372 N.W. 2d 738 (M.I. 1982).

Klein Independent School District v. Mattox, 830 F., 2d 576 (5th Cir. 1987).

Krauss v. Nassau Community College, 469 N.Y.S. 2d 553 (S.Ct. Sp. Term, Nassau 1983).

Kryston v. Board of Ed. East Ramapo, Etc., 430 N.Y.S. 2d 688 (App. Div. 2nd Dept. 1980).

Lemon v. Kurtzman, 403 U.S. 601 (1971).

Olsson v. Indiana Univ. Bd. of Trustees, 571 N.E. 2d 585 (Ind. App. 4th Dist. 1991).

Price v. Young, 580 F. Supp. 1 (E.D. Ark. W.D. 1983).

Red and Black Pub. Co., Inc. v. Board of Regents, 427 S.E. 2d 257 (Ga. 1993).

The Shreveport Professional Chapter of the Society of Professional Journalists and Michelle Millhollon v. Louisiana State University in Shreveport. No. 393,332 (First Judicial District Court, Caddo Parish, La. 1994).

Smith v. Duquesne University, 612 F. Supp. 72 (W.D. Pa. Civil 1985).

Spas v. Wharton, 431 N.Y.S. 2d 638 (S. Ct. Albany 1980).

State v. Birdsall, 568 P. 2d 1094 (Az. App. 1977).

Stone v. Cornell University, 510 N.Y.S. 29 2d 313 (App. Div. 1987).

Student Bar Ass'n. Bd. of Governors, Etc. v. Byrd, 239 S.E. 2d 415 (N.C. 1977).

Tarka v. Cunningham, 741 F. Supp. 1281 (W.D. Texas, Austin 1990).

Tarka v. Franklin, 891 F. 2d 102 (5th Cir. 1989).

DONALD D. GEHRING *is professor of higher education and student affairs and director of the higher education doctoral program at Bowling Green State University.*

This chapter attempts to help readers understand federal policy, develop strategies for complying with federal mandates, and examine selected issues associated with compliance with federal policy.

Implementing Federal Policy on Campus

John H. Schuh, Tracy Y. Ogle

Over the past quarter century, the federal government has become involved with the daily business of colleges and universities at an accelerating rate. If one considers such federal initiatives as the Family Educational Rights and Privacy Act (FERPA), Section 504 of the Rehabilitation Act of 1973, Title IX of the Education Amendments of 1972, and the Crime Awareness and Campus Security Act of 1990, one easily can reach the conclusion that higher education is becoming a highly regulated enterprise. The federal government regulates such routine campus activities as how student records are handled (FERPA), the minimum wage students can earn while working on campus (Fair Labor Standards Act, as amended), the structure of an intercollegiate athletics program (Title IX), and the conditions under which the school band can play certain tunes and students can watch videocassettes in a residence hall lounge (Copyright Law of 1976).

Whether one agrees or disagrees with these initiatives is beside the point. They are the law, and colleges and universities must comply with them. Often, the initial reaction to these mandates is that the federal government has no business intruding into the daily operation of institutions of higher education. According to this line of thinking, these intrusions demand expensive responses in times of extremely limited financial resources, and they place an unreasonable burden on institutions. Moreover, some of the regulations seem to require the obvious, such as informing students and faculty that the possession and use of illicit drugs is against the law. Although these reactions are genuine and perhaps accurate depending on one's perspective and politics, it also is important to remember that the values that many of these mandates purport to emphasize, such as open access and equity, are consistent with what student affairs officers have adopted as their own philosophy. For example, *A Perspective on Student Affairs,* adopted by NASPA in celebration of the fiftieth anniversary of the Student Personnel Point of View, states, "Each student is unique, yet all students should be treated equitably (Committee for a New Century, 1989, p. 18).

Faced with the additional activities required by federal legislation, student affairs administrators have two choices: ignore federal mandates or determine how to comply. Because the first is not really a choice for those who wish to remain employed, student affairs officers are well advised to develop strategies to comply with federal legislation. Indeed, as Gehring (1993) reports, "Student affairs practitioners . . . can ill afford not to listen to what the law has to say. Though administrators need not be lawyers, their failure to understand and stay abreast of legal implications in developing and administering programs, policies and practices can have devastating consequences for themselves, the institution, and the students" (p. 274).

Higher education administrators should not feel they are alone in dealing with increased federal intrusion in their daily activities. The federal government during the previous decade has shifted responsibility to the states for a variety of governmental activities, including hazardous waste removal, health care, welfare, and housing. (See Schuh, 1993.) One observer gave this example: "Medicaid was originally envisioned as a partnership between states and the federal government. In recent years, major changes in federal requirements have become more frequent and are often costly for the states to implement" (Dubin, 1992, p. 7).

Policy mandates that affect higher education are not easy to implement and institutions are not anxious to comply. As Stoker (1991, p. 4) indicates, "The challenge of national governance is to gain the cooperation of *reluctant partners:* implementation participants who enjoy substantial autonomy and whose cooperation is uncertain and may be difficult to achieve." It would hardly be an exercise in hyperbole to claim that many institutions of higher education reluctantly cooperate with the federal government in implementing mandates that require time, effort, and financial resources in compliance activities.

At times, federal regulations appear to conflict with each other. For example, FERPA protects the official records of students, including records related to student disciplinary hearings. However, without amending FERPA, the Sexual Assault Victim's Bill of Rights requires that victims of sexual assaults committed by other students must be informed of campus hearings against the alleged perpetrators. Janes (1988) points out that FERPA and the regulations of the Immigration and Naturalization Service also may conflict with each other.

This chapter is designed to present strategies to help the student affairs administrator comply with and implement various federal policies. Three areas will be discussed, including understanding the requirements of federal law and administrative regulations, developing strategies to implement responses appropriate to federal mandates, and addressing contemporary issues and concerns about federal policy.

However, this chapter should not be considered definitive. Rather, its intent is to discuss briefly the topics listed and to provide suggestions for responding to federal law. Because each institution has unique resources and organizational properties, student affairs administrators are urged to work with the college's legal counsel, governmental relations staff, and others who are familiar with federal law and campus idiosyncrasies. If we are able to encourage readers to sharpen their thinking about this complex topic, then we will have been successful in our effort. We also note that we use the terms *college* and *university* synonymously in this chapter. Each refers to an institution of higher education without regard to size, curriculum, or complexity.

Understanding Federal Law

Before determining what actions to take to meet the expectations of a federal law, student affairs administrators have to find out about the law and understand its requirements. Several good sources for this information are available on many campuses although they may not be a part of the structure of every college. Indeed, very small, independent colleges may not have an office of governmental relations while a large university can be so complicated in an organizational sense that it may be difficult to determine just who has the responsibility for compliance with federal mandates. Nonetheless, several sources exist on many campuses and we will describe each of them briefly.

Governmental Relations Officer. Many campuses have a senior administrator who is charged with working with various governmental agencies and monitoring legislative developments. Commonly, this person is not located in the division of student affairs. (See Sandeen, 1989.) The responsibilities of the governmental relations officer can range from such activities as working with local governmental agencies and coordinating the institution's legislative relations program to working with representatives and senators in Washington.

This person should be aware of potential federal initiatives, know members of legislative and congressional staffs, and read such publications as the *Federal Register.* The governmental relations officer will provide a first line of information about legislation in the works and laws just after they are passed.

Legal Counsel. Once a law has been enacted, student affairs officers will need help in understanding what the law requires. Campus administrators are cautioned not to try to practice the law. As Gehring (1993) points out, "The specific facts, the current state of the law, and the private or public nature of the institution of higher education all will influence the legal aspects of student affairs. Competent legal advice is necessary and should be sought" (p. 294). Legal counsel can be very helpful in explaining what the institution needs to accomplish to respond to the requirements. Legal counsel can be especially helpful in reviewing language included in brochures, catalogs, and other documents that could at a later date be construed as terms of a contract.

Consortia. In some cases, institutions (often private or independent) are not large enough to sustain their own governmental relations office or full-time legal counsel. Consortia have been developed so that resources such as attorneys or legislative specialists can be shared. In this way, student affairs officers can work together to understand how to respond to various federal mandates.

Professional Associations. Professional associations such as NASPA and ACPA publish periodic newsletters that identify federal initiatives while they are in the process of being formulated. NASPA publishes a regular column on legal issues and the federal scene in its newsletter, the *NASPA Forum.* The reader also is referred to the *NASFAA Newsletter* and the *NASFAA Federal Monitor.* These materials can be extremely helpful. They acquaint the student affairs officer with federal initiatives as they are being developed and recommend following up with staff discussions about how to comply with the specific federal mandate.

Using these sources, as well as personal contacts in various governmental agencies at both the state and federal level, student affairs officers should be able to develop an understanding of federal mandates and the responses required of them. A list of additional resources is provided in Chapter Seven.

Implementing Federal Policy

After becoming familiar with a new federal law, regulation, administrative regulation or ruling, the next step is to develop strategies for complying with it. This section will describe several activities that student affairs officers and others on campus should consider in responding to new federal requirements. Four types of mandates will be discussed briefly: changes in facilities, policies, programs, and information distribution.

The first matter that needs to be taken care of is deciding who is responsible for seeing that the institution is in compliance with the federal mandate. We believe that because entire institutions are affected by penalties related to noncompliance (such as the withdrawal of federal funding for a broad variety of institutional activities), compliance is everybody's responsibility. Clearly, some units should be assigned to provide leadership for organizing compliance activities. But, even if the registrar, for example, is charged with overseeing FERPA compliance, the judicial affairs office has as much responsibility for appropriate record keeping as the registrar does.

As a result of their study of mandated academic change, Newcombe and Conrad (1981) conclude, "The importance of institutional leaders, particularly college presidents, in implementing a mandate should not be underestimated" (p. 573). As these mandates are handed down by the federal government, senior institutional leaders of colleges and universities should be familiar with what they require, make the resources available to put the appropriate institutional response in place, and provide leadership so that the response is completed in a manner consistent with the institution's mission and values. The chief student affairs officer also should be well informed and knowledgeable about federal mandates. Sandeen (1991, p. 76) observes that "issues such as student financial aid . . . housing loans, disabled student programs, . . . crime reporting requirements, and student confidentiality laws are critical to the institution, and the CSAO should be the best informed administrator on campus regarding them."

We believe that too often compliance activities are seen as "somebody else's problem" and shuffled off to as low an administrative level as possible. That is a mistake. Compliance with mandates ought to be viewed as an institutional matter, with many aspects of the college contributing to the effort to place the institution in compliance. Student affairs, of course, will play an important role in many of these activities.

Facility Issues. An important, ongoing response required of institutions has been to make physical facilities accessible to all students. Section 504 introduced this concept, the Americans with Disabilities Act reinforced it, and together, they provide an excellent opportunity for various institutional staff to work together to address a federal mandate regarding access to facilities. What the mandate means, at least in theory, is that all persons ought to have access to all facilities (and programs and activities) on the campus. How access is defined and facilitated is the subject of vigorous debate in many circumstances, but the concept remains in place.

Who might be involved in an institution's effort to make physical facilities accessible? A number of key players should be a part of this activity, including the director of services for the physically challenged, the architect of the institution, legal counsel, facilities planning staff, physical plant staff, the affirmative action officer, the 504 compliance officer, the ADA coordinator, and those responsible for each campus building. Modifications to existing facilities can be very expensive, and there may be a tendency to wait to begin work until a complaint is received. This strategy, however, is short-sighted. Institutional representatives, including those mentioned, and disabled individuals should work together to develop comprehensive plans to make sure that facilities are accessible in a permanent sense.

However, this will result in only a partial solution. When facilities are modified for specific activities outside their normal use pattern—for example, modifying a football stadium for use in commencement exercises—the event planner's checklist should also include making sure that it is accessible to everyone who will be using it. If diplomas are to be awarded on a stage, can people in wheelchairs get to the stage? Will the sound system be adequate for those with hearing impairments? Will an interpreter be required? Such questions have to be addressed every time a facility is used for a special purpose.

Program Issues. A second area where alliances need to be formed involves the college's academic and nonacademic programs. Depending on the specific program, student affairs administrators, academic administrators, faculty, legal counsel, facility planners, and perhaps others, depending on the nature of the program, will need to be brought together to make sure that federal mandates are addressed in a satisfactory manner.

Title IX is an example of how a federal mandate has affected programs. It prohibits discrimination "on the basis of sex . . . under any educational program or activity receiving federal financial assistance" (20 U.S.C. 1681). Such activities as admissions, housing, health care, counseling, and athletics (including intercollegiate and club sports) are affected by the law. Until passage of this law, many intercollegiate sports programs, and, we suspect, club sport programs as well, had substantially greater funds available in support of men's activities than women's activities. Kaplin (1985) identifies ten areas that lead to equality in intercollegiate athletics for men and women. Although progress in addressing this highly charged mandate has been made, work still needs to be completed.

Athletic administrators and coaches have had to rethink and restructure their programs to meet Title IX regulations to provide equal equipment, travel and per diem allowances, medical services, publicity, game scheduling, and housing and dining services. Thus Title IX has had a significant effect on how intercollegiate athletics programs are structured and has provided far better opportunities for women in this area of college life than existed before passage of the law.

Policy Issues. Some federal mandates influence institutional policy. One of the best examples is FERPA. FERPA has had an effect on every institutional office that handles an "official" student record. Grades, obviously, are official university records and, as a result, every faculty member who awards grades has an obligation to understand the law and adhere to it. As much damage can be done to an institution by faculty who fail to adhere to FERPA regulations as by faculty who are sloppy in their handling of records in university offices.

Collaboration across various divisions of the institution is essential in compliance with a mandate like FERPA. Such institutional activities as properly instructing new faculty who handle student grades, working with clerical and secretarial people who physically handle records, developing computer safeguards to protect electronic records, and working with others involved in the record keeping of the institution, must be accomplished.

An example of a more recent federal mandate that has resulted in policy development is the requirement—of the Higher Education Amendments of 1992—that, beginning in fall 1993, institutions distribute information including the college's sexual assault policy. Institutional officers first had to decide if the institutional policies that were in place before the act was signed were adequate, if they needed to be modified, or if new policies had to be promulgated. The development or modification of a sexual assault policy involves law enforcement officers, legal counsel, student affairs staff, advocates for women, faculty, and students. The enforcement and oversight of such a policy ordinarily would fall to law enforcement officials and student affairs staff. However, policy development cuts across many institutional boundaries and should involve many constituents because it has the potential to be highly charged in a political sense.

Informational Programs. A fairly recent development in the federal mandate scene is the obligation for institutions of higher education to provide information to students and others about graduation rates, substance abuse programs, and criminal activity (a result of the Drug Free Schools and Communities Act Amendments of 1989 and Crime and Awareness and Campus Security Act of 1990). Each student and employee has to be provided with information, such as a description of illegal substances, laws related to substance abuse, annual crime statistics, and the institution's alcohol possession and consumption policy, on an annual basis.

The development and distribution of material to comply with these laws requires collaboration from many institutional representatives, again including law enforcement, student affairs, legal counsel, university publications, registration, and others, depending on the nature of the information. (For example, counseling and health center staff would need to provide information about the availability of treatment programs for persons with substance abuse problems.) In each case, the requirements of the mandate have to be examined before determining who needs to be involved and to what extent.

Further, the development of an adequate institutional response requires thoughtful planning well in advance of when the material needs to be distributed. The distribution process itself may not be easy, especially for institutions where a substantial number of students do not live in campus residence halls. Distribution by publishing the information in the campus newspaper or even in the schedule of classes generally is considered inadequate to comply with the law. The federal government requires personalized distribution of the material in writing to individual students and faculty.

A Theory of Mandated Academic Change. Newcombe and Conrad present a theory about mandated academic change that helps sum up the activities identified in the previous section. They indicate that implementation of federal mandates involves a four-step process. We describe this process briefly in this section of this chapter (Newcombe and Conrad, 1981).

Infusion. In this first step, the mandate is introduced to the institution and its meaning for various constituencies is determined.

Preparation and Policy Formulation. In this step, administrators and others formulate plans for change. Administrative units are identified to facilitate compliance efforts.

Trial and Transition. During this stage, a recognizable course of action is identified, and formal policy on implementing the mandate is established, clarified, and articulated.

Policy Execution. In this final step, the policy is gradually accepted and implemented.

The reader is encouraged to read the entire study, which includes an analysis of the implementation of policies in response to Title IX at thirteen four-year public colleges and universities in Virginia.

Evaluation Techniques. After the institution's response to the federal mandate has been implemented, the institution is well advised to develop a strategy to evaluate the effectiveness of its response. The nature of the evaluation will depend to a great extent on the federal mandate, its requirements for the institution, and, perhaps most importantly, the effect of the response on constituents. An excellent place to start the evaluation is to determine the extent to which the goals and objectives of the institution's response met the needs of students (Miller and Winston, 1991). One example of an evaluation of mandated services is provided by Schuh and Veltman (1991).

Related Issues

It is important that student affairs administrators are familiar with a few of the long-term issues associated with the implementation of federal policy on campus. Two that are likely to continue to affect administrators in the foreseeable future are increased regulatory involvement, and—in keeping with the trend of shifting costs to state and local governments—a shift in responsibility for the costs of implementing mandates from the government to the colleges.

Increased Federal Involvement. According to the Advisory Commission on Intergovernmental Relations (ACIR), an independent commission created by the federal government, "State and local governments, like the business sector and private individuals, have been affected greatly by the massive extension of federal controls and standards over the past two decades" (1992, p. 5).

One reason that increased federal involvement has become an important issue is that it has been viewed by the higher education community as infringing on its traditional autonomy. The intrusion of the federal government into traditional realms of educational governance often has been a source of friction.

Another area of concern is the federal government's perceived inflexibility. The ACIR concludes, "Where the federal government once encouraged state and local actions with fiscal incentives, it now also wields sanctions—or simply issues commands" (1992, p. 5). The federal government has spent little effort in trying to understand the unique circumstances of many campuses and the extraordinary efforts campuses have undertaken to meet mandated requirements. For example, to comply with regulations about information dissemination, commuter institutions must mail the material to each student, because most do not live in campus residence halls and thus do not have mailboxes on campus. No relief is provided for the expense of mailing materials to thousands of students. The federal government simply threatens to attach huge fines or to withdraw funding for specific programs if the regulations are not met.

Shift in Responsibility. In 1992, then-president George Bush directly addressed this problem in his State of the Union address: "We must put an end to unfinanced federal government mandates . . . . If Congress passes a mandate, it should be forced to pay for it and balance the cost with savings elsewhere" (cited by Conlan and Beam, 1992, p. 7). Although acknowledging the problem, the Congressional Budget Office (CBO) concluded in an estimate of intergovernmental fiscal effects of proposed federal legislation that "federally mandated costs have risen rapidly since 1986, growing at a pace faster than overall federal aid" (Conlan and Beam, 1992, p. 9). The rising costs of federal mandates are a highly visible concern for many student affairs administrators, especially during times of severe fiscal constraints.

The varying costs of compliance make it extremely difficult to measure accurately the cost of governmental regulation in higher education. For example, an analysis at Wichita State University for the 1993 fiscal year estimated the costs of compliance with federal mandates to total approximately $1.4 million (R. Lowe, personal communication, June 29, 1993). The estimated cost for the division of student affairs alone was approximately $332,000 out of a total operating budget of nearly $7 million. Viewed another way, about 4.6 percent of the total student affairs operating budget was spent on compliance with federal regulations.

Another reason for the difficulty in determining the actual cost of compliance is that many of the goals of federally mandated programs are consistent with the philosophy of student affairs administrators, and possibly would have been initiated regardless of a federal mandate. Although many federal regulations address important problems that have been identified previously by many campuses, too often the funds necessary to address them are committed to other needs. And, unfortunately, the days when the federal government offered fiscal incentives have been succeeded by unfunded federal mandates. Congress simply passes the expense on to an already-strained campus budget.

Thus, student affairs administrators are justified in their concerns. The Sloan Commission on Government and Higher Education states that "government regulation of higher education is a permanent feature of modern society" and relief for campuses will only come if they "build on existing mandate monitoring efforts and devote much more sustained attention to influencing the formulation of federal regulations" (Edwards, 1980, pp. 9, 15).

Colleges and universities have not been as effective as they might be in making the case that they will meet the objectives of proposed mandates through voluntary compliance. Until that happens, institutions of higher education can anticipate additional regulation without the attendant funding to support it.

References

Advisory Committee on Intergovernmental Relations. "Federal Regulation of State and Local Government: A Status Report." *Intergovernmental Perspective,* 1992, *18*(4), 5–6.

Committee for a New Century. "A Perspective on Student Affairs." In NASPA (ed.), *Points of View.* Washington, D.C.: NASPA, 1989.

Conlan, T. J., and Beam, D. R. "Federal Mandates: The Record of Reform and Future Prospects." *Intergovernmental Perspective,* 1992, *18*(4), 7–11.

Dubin, E. J. "Medicaid Reform: Major Trends and Issues." *Intergovernmental Perspective,* 1992, *18*(2), 5–9.

Edwards, H. T. *Higher Education and the Unholy Crusade Against Governmental Regulation.* Cambridge, Mass.: Harvard Institute for Education Management, 1980.

Gehring, D. D. "Understanding Legal Constraints." In M. J. Barr and Associates (eds.), *The Handbook of Student Affairs Administration.* San Francisco: Jossey-Bass, 1993.

Janes, S. S. "Administrative Practice: A Day-to-Day Guide to Legal Requirements." In M. J. Barr and Associates (eds.), *The Handbook of Student Affairs Administration.* San Francisco: Jossey-Bass, 1988.

Kaplin, W. A. *The Law of Higher Education.* (2nd ed.) San Francisco: Jossey-Bass, 1985.

Miller, T. K., and Winston, R. B., Jr. "Human Development and Higher Education." In T. K. Miller and R. B. Winston (eds.), *Administration and Leadership in Student Affairs.* Muncie, Ind.: Accelerated Development, 1991.

Newcombe, J. P., and Conrad, C. F. "A Theory of Mandated Academic Change." *Journal of Higher Education,* 1981, 52 (6), 555–577.

Sandeen, A. "Issues Influencing the Organization of Student Affairs." In. U. Delworth and G. R. Hanson (eds.), *Student Services: A Handbook for the Profession.* San Francisco: Jossey-Bass, 1989.

Sandeen, A. *The Chief Student Affairs Officer.* San Francisco: Jossey-Bass, 1991.

Schuh, J. H. "Fiscal Pressures on Higher Education and Student Affairs." In M. J. Barr (ed.), *Student Affairs Administration.* San Francisco: Jossey-Bass, 1993.

Schuh, J. H., and Veltman, G. C. "Application of an Ecosystem Model to an Office of Handicapped Services." *Journal of College Student Development,* 1991, 32 (3), 236–240.

Stoker, R. P. *Reluctant Partners: Implementing Federal Policy.* Pittsburgh, Penn.: University of Pittsburgh Press, 1991.

JOHN H. SCHUH is associate vice president for student affairs and professor of counseling and school psychology at Wichita State University. He has been recognized by NASPA and ACPA for his contributions to the student affairs literature.

TRACY Y. OGLE is an adjunct instructor at Butler County Community College in Kansas. She has served as an intern in the Office of Student Life at Wichita State University where she completed her master's degree in public administration. She also has been a residence halls administrator at Wichita State University.

The aggressive implementation of federal laws and regulations affecting higher education threaten a homogenization of higher education creating a federal university.

The Federal University

Donald D. Gehring

> Mankind are more disposed to suffer, while evils are sufferable, than to right themselves by abolishing the forms to which they are accustomed.
>
> —The Declaration of Independence

In 1927, the United States Supreme Court held that a warrantless wiretap of an individual's telephone did not violate the Fourth Amendment guarantee that the people shall be secure in their persons, houses, papers, and effects against unreasonable searches and seizures. The wiretap was designed to obtain evidence against an individual who was transporting and selling intoxicating liquors during Prohibition. Justice Louis Brandeis dissented from that opinion, saying it was "immaterial that the intrusion was in aid of law enforcement. Experience should teach us to be most on our guard to protect liberty when the government's purposes are beneficent. Men born to freedom are naturally alert to repel invasion of their liberty by evil-minded rulers. The greatest dangers to liberty lurk in insidious encroachment by men of zeal, well-meaning, but without understanding" (*Olmstead v. United States,* 277 U.S. 438 at 480, 1927).

This year, as we celebrate the thirtieth anniversary of the Higher Education Act of 1965, the most comprehensive federal law affecting higher education, we need to be mindful of Justice Brandeis's warning and to be on guard to protect our liberty.

Thus far this monograph has provided an introduction to the historical evolution of federal involvement in higher education; an orientation to the federal policy process; a discussion of various laws and regulations that mandate specific actions that student affairs and other campus administrators must take in developing programs, policies, and plans; and suggestions for devising campus responses to those policies. This chapter provides an analysis of federal legislative involvement and a critique of the federal rule making process. This critique is based on the author's firsthand knowledge and interaction with the regulatory process for more than twenty years and is supported by other authorities in the field. It is not intended to focus on or diminish the many positive benefits of federal legislation that has attempted to eliminate discrimination and the debilitating effects of drugs and alcohol and that has been intended to provide student consumers the information necessary to make informed choices. Rather, the chapter examines the cost of those benefits. Furthermore, it provides suggestions for influencing the legislative and regulatory processes.

Although historically higher education has enjoyed a positive relationship with and fared well financially at the hands of the federal government, the purpose of this chapter is to examine critically federal involvement in higher education. Although our government is well intentioned and its laws beneficent, without a critical understanding of federal laws and their regulations, we may fail to recognize how our liberty and the values that sustain higher education are being eroded by their intrusion.

Since this monograph is directed primarily to student affairs administrators, the laws and regulations discussed and the examples used are primarily those related directly to student affairs work. Many other federal laws control and direct other activities of colleges and universities, such as Title VII, Executive Order 11246 as amended by Executive Order 11375, Research and Human Subjects, Age Discrimination in Education Act, and the Vietnam Era Veterans Readjustment Act. There are many examples in these areas that parallel those discussed in the chapter; however, they are not included because of space limitations.

Higher Education as a Vehicle of Federal Policy

A critical understanding of federal law requires a recognition that laws affecting higher education were not necessarily designed to enhance or improve higher education but rather to fulfill national social or economic goals (Fleming, 1978). Senator Moynihan recognized this axiom in 1975 when he singled out the 1958 National Defense Education Act and "equal opportunity grants" to make the following observation:

> Once again higher education policy was deployed by the national government to serve external political needs, in this case to press further to fill out a central theme of the Kennedy and Johnson administration—that of equality. For the space of eight years between those two bills the direction of federal policy toward higher education was all but reversed, going from excellence to universalism . . . . Higher education was a means of obtaining goals elsewhere in the political system (Moynihan, 1975, p. 153).

Although most academics would agree that the primary purposes of higher education are teaching, research, and public service, they would not recognize the fourth mission—serving as a vehicle for the implementation of federal policy. Higher education has been used by government in this way since the early days of the republic and continues to be used in this way even today (Fleming, 1978).

In 1785 the population was centered in the East. In order to encourage movement into the northwest territories of the new republic, Congress included a provision in the Land Ordinances of 1785 setting aside a lot in every township for the maintenance of education (Rainsford, 1972).

Later, when the Morrill Act was introduced, its initial impetus was not to develop a system of state universities but rather to dispose of federal lands and appease the nation's farmers, who constituted about 45 percent of the free male population and were becoming increasingly vocal about their educational needs (Brubacher and Rudy, 1968; Rainsford, 1972; Rudolph, 1990; Williams, 1991). In order to satisfy both the northern and recently reunited southern constituents, Congress enacted the second Morrill Act in 1890, which contained a "separate but equal" provision that created problems that continue to plague higher education. Although no federal funds would be made available under the act to states or territories "where a distinction of race or color is made in the admission of students," the provision would be satisfied by having separate facilities for African American youth if the funds were divided on a "just and equitable" basis (Rainsford, 1972). It is also of interest to note that when the original Morrill Act was passed in 1862 the nation was at war, and the act required that the curriculum of land grant institutions include training in military tactics.

During World War I, Congress, again recognizing the need for trained manpower, saw colleges and universities as a vehicle to accomplish this end. The National Defense Act of 1916 provided for, among other things, the creation of ROTC units on campuses across the country.

As World War II was winding down, the government once again looked to colleges and universities as a source of implementing federal social policy. Two serious social problems would need to be confronted at the end of the war. The first involved the economic impact on the nation of the infusion into the workforce of thousands of returning servicemen, probably leading to unemployment and the consequent possibility of a new depression. A somewhat related problem, and potentially even more serious, was the likelihood of large numbers of well-trained, unemployed, and dissatisfied veterans marching on Washington, as their predecessors after World War I had done. The veterans of World War I who marched on Washington, known as the Bonus Expeditionary Force, had occupied vacant buildings, set up huts on vacant property, and clashed with police before being driven out of Washington by four companies of infantry and cavalry commanded by Douglas MacArthur. Although no one was killed and only a few were hurt in that early skirmish, the planners in 1942 were not sure they would be as fortunate if the well-trained veterans of World War II converged on Washington demanding jobs

(Ross, 1969). Thus the planners developed the GI Bill, which kept veterans busy and out of the labor market.

In 1958, when the Soviets launched Sputnik, President Eisenhower recommended an expansion of the National Science Foundation and several new initiatives to improve science education. These initiatives became known as the National Defense Education Act of 1958 and were seen as a way "to counter the Soviet achievements in scientific manpower training and research" (Wilson, 1983, p. 45).

Thus federal support of higher education programs is directed toward ends other than developing the national resource of higher education. Further, "federal officials authorizing and administering the programs do not regard support of colleges and universities as anything but an artifact of expenditures directed toward other national objectives" (Finn, 1978, p. 106). The 1960s and 1970s were dubbed by one commentator as the period when higher education became a national social laboratory. It was during those years when most social legislation was passed, including Title VI of the Civil Rights Act, the Education Amendment of 1972 (including Title IX), the Rehabilitation Act of 1973 (including Section 504), and the Elementary and Secondary Act of 1974 (containing FERPA). These laws and the more current legislation of the late 1980s and the 1990s often reflect the personal values and judgments of very few members of Congress and lobbyists who believe the legislation should be enacted (Sumberg, 1978; Finn, 1978). It is hard to believe that Congress would have passed a Campus Security Act without a strong lobby effort funded by the parents of a coed who was raped and murdered on a college campus. Likewise, the Drug Free Schools and Communities Act Amendments of 1989 would probably not be legislation today if not for the efforts of then-secretary of education William Bennett, who was successful in using his office as a "bully pulpit" (DeLoughry, 1989; Gladieux and Lewis, 1987).

A Loss of Trust

Although the federal government uses higher education as a vehicle to accomplish other social and political goals, few in higher education would disagree with those goals, especially when higher education itself has benefited from the legislation. "It is not the law's operation per se that troubles the critic; it is the jeopardy in which law places cherished values that causes alarm" (Hobbs, 1978a, p. 3). To be sure, many lament the intrusion of the government into higher education as a loss of autonomy while others view it as an added expense and inefficiency during economically hard times; still others believe it is creating an adversarial relationship between our government and our colleges and universities (Finn, 1978; Seabury, 1979b; Palmer, Gehring, and Guthrie, 1992; Wilson, 1983; Hobbs, 1978b; Editorial Projects for Education, 1979). However, few if any would be opposed to ensuring equal opportunity, improving science education, protecting the privacy of students' records, or combating the debilitating effects of drugs and alcohol. United States Court of

Appeals Judge Harry Edwards has observed, "Many of the objections posed by critics are to the *procedures* used to implement federal regulations rather than the *principles* of the legislation" (Edwards, 1980, p. 16). However, it is not the procedures alone that are objectional; even more objectionable is the jeopardy in which those procedures have placed our cherished trust. This loss of trust in government and the adversarial relationship it fosters are the real tragedies of federal regulation of higher education. We must therefore be on guard to protect our liberties from "the insidious encroachment by men of zeal, well meaning but without understanding" (*Olmsted v. United States,* 1927).

The lack of trust is born not from paranoia but from thousands of examples of broken promises and overly aggressive rule making and enforcement by zealous bureaucrats. Chester Finn, a former research associate at the Brookings Institute, has summarized his arguments concerning federal intrusion into the affairs of higher education by saying, "In a word, federal control is illegal" (Finn, 1978, p. 140). Estelle Fishbein, general counsel for Johns Hopkins University, has characterized federal regulation of higher education as "vastly *more* dangerous than the McCarthyism of the fifties" (Fishbein, 1978, p. 58).

To understand how the trust has been broken, one must first understand how the federal government becomes involved in higher education. The term "education" is never mentioned in the United States Constitution, and the Tenth Amendment provides that "The powers not delegated to the United States by the Constitution, nor prohibited by it to the States, are reserved to the States respectively, or to the people." However, under Article I, Section 8 of the Constitution, Congress has the power to "lay and collect taxes, . . . [and] provide for the common defense and general welfare." Thus Congress may provide funding to higher education as a means of providing for the general welfare. Obviously, Congress would have the right to specify how funds thus provided are spent. Therefore, many in government and higher education have been fearful of providing federal dollars to higher education lest it be subject to federal control. Senator Barry Goldwater sounded the warning in 1958 during debates on the NDEA when he said, "If adopted, this legislation will mark the inception of aid, supervision, and ultimately control of education in this country by federal authorities" (Weinberger, 1979, p. 47).

Later, a number of federal programs were brought under one piece of umbrella legislation known as the Higher Education Act of 1965. To allay the fears of college administrators that accepting funds under the act would subject them to federal control, the act contained a provision known as section 1144(a), which succinctly stated: "Nothing contained in this chapter shall be construed to authorize any department, agency, officer, or employee of the United States to exercise any direction, supervision, or control over the curriculum, programs of instruction, administration, or personnel of any educational institution."

Although this section was subsequently repealed, it was replaced by the General Education Provisions Act (20 U.S.C. § 1232a), which prohibits the same supervision, direction, and control by federal agencies under every provision of "any applicable program."

This is the reason Finn (1978) found federal control to be illegal. When this point was raised with a representative of the Department of Health, Education, and Welfare (DHEW) at a meeting in Atlanta designed to explain Title IX regulations, the representative replied that by implementing the regulations her agency was not exercising any direction, supervision, or control over any curriculum, program of instruction, administration, or personnel, but merely saying that if we didn't operate our curriculum and administer our programs of instruction the way DHEW said to, it would take all our federal funds away (Gehring, personal communication, July 15, 1975). Her artful semantics and arrogant response represented a careful, well thought out, and probably planned argument that met strict legal parameters but violated the basic intent of the laws, and created the lack of trust and adversarial relationship between higher education and government that continues to plague us today.

Certainly federal agencies have a difficult task in writing regulations to implement congressional intent. This is especially true when "Congress intentionally fudged in the law itself" (Bailey, 1978, p. 106) or was silent on a point (Sumberg, 1978). However, the problem of rule making is also exacerbated by the one-size-fits-all theory. Higher education institutions differ significantly in this country. Yet when rules are written, in most cases, they are applied with equal force to proprietary and tax-supported, religiously affiliated and state, large and small, and rural and urban institutions. Furthermore, regulating higher education should be a very different process from regulating business and industry since "manufacturers and retail establishments may be regulated and constricted, yet the business of production and buying and selling can still go on. But if regulation of the university inhibits inquiry, if it suppresses the free expression of intellectual judgment and the responsible exercise of discretion, then the business of the university is concluded" (Fishbein, 1978, p. 59).

Recognizing the unique and complex nature of higher education institutions in our society and the significant contributions these institutions make would seem to call for careful and cautious planning, including consultation with campus administrators to develop an understanding of the impact laws would have on both individual campuses and higher education as a whole. Although this type of planning would logically precede the development of laws and rules, this has not been the case. Higher education groups did not even appear to testify before adoption of Title IX (Advisory Commission on Intergovernmental Relations, 1981).

The Family Educational Rights and Privacy Act (20 U.S.C. 1232g) was a floor amendment to the Elementary and Secondary Act of 1974 and was never even subject to committee hearings. The amendment was based on problems discovered with the privacy of student records at the elementary and secondary level, yet higher education was included in the Act as an afterthought (Advisory Commission on Intergovernmental Relations, 1981). Higher education was thus not given an opportunity to inform Congress that most postsecondary institutions were already giving students access to their records and that they were almost unanimously denying access to unauthorized members of the campus (Dutton, Smith, and Zarle, 1969).

Because of Senator Buckley's ill-conceived, hastily and poorly planned bill, modifications of the act were subsequently required and courts are still not in agreement about its intent. (Compare *Red and Black Publishing Company, Inc. v. Board of Regents*, 1993 with *The Shreveport Professional Chapter of the Society of Professional Journalists and Michelle Millhollon v. Louisiana State University in Shreveport*, 1994.) The passage of FERPA was not an isolated instance of congressional failure to understand higher education. In 1873, *The Nation* published an article decrying the "stupendous ignorance of Congress in matters of education" (Williams, 1991, p. 72). Congress has not only failed to understand higher education but has also become very aggressive in its control of it. Everyone would agree that if you want to dance you must pay the piper; Congress has the right to control the expenditure of federal funds. But Congress has taken an aggressive stance that extends beyond the mere control of tax dollars. Congress now controls institutions' actions in areas funded by private dollars. If an institution receives one cent in any area, it must comply with federal mandates in all areas (P.L. 100–259). Yet Congress had promised that if institutions took its funding to accomplish federal objectives, it would not exercise control—another chip in the wall of trust.

The ignorance often displayed by Congress is matched only by the aggressiveness of bureaucrats who often do not follow congressional intent in writing rules. Bureaucratic aggressiveness, too, is not a new phenomenon. When the House Committee on Education and Labor sent a series of questions to land grant institutions to determine whether the colleges were fulfilling their obligations under the 1862 Morrill Act, it was characterized by one professor as "unfriendly in motive and in aim" (Williams, 1991, p. 76). More recently the relationship between government and higher education has been described as "one of high suspicion and distrust" (Wilson, 1983, p. viii), "adversarial" (Ketter, 1978), and "an adversary relationship at best and open hostility at worst" (Editorial Projects for Education, 1979).

This debilitating relationship can be attributed in part to higher education's own intransigence. The academy did discriminate against racial and ethnic minorities, and women and disabled persons, and laws may have been needed to correct these inequities, although there were other ways to solve these problems. However, more recently it has been the arrogance and aggressiveness of agency bureaucrats that has fostered the suspicion and hostility. Even a former secretary of education recognized that the Office of Civil Rights (OCR) was overly aggressive in enforcing its regulations and displayed a tendency to charge colleges with violations of regulations even before the institutions had a reasonable opportunity to comply (Winkler, 1981). Senator Bayh, one of the sponsors of Title IX, said that DHEW had "gone out of its way to pick some of the most ridiculous examples of the intention of Title IX" ("Senate Approves Higher Vocational Education Bill," 1976, p. 1).

Congresswoman Edith Green, the author of Title IX said: "If I or others in the House had argued that this legislation was designed to do some of the things which HEW now says it was designed to do, I believe the legislation would have been defeated. I myself would not have voted for it, even though I feel very strongly about ending discrimination on the basis of sex (cited in Bennett, 1976, p. 130).

The Justice Department charged Brigham Young University with violating the Fair Housing Act (42 U.S.C. §3601, et seq.) because "BYU has caused land-lords to segregate their apartment buildings on the basis of sex as a condition of being eligible to house BYU students" (Department of Justice letter DJ 175–77–22, Feb. 28, 1978). The Department of Justice did not even have the courtesy to inform Dallin Oaks, the president of the university, first. Rather, it first sent a copy of its letter of a proposed lawsuit against BYU to the media, which in turn gave a copy to President Oaks. In his response, which he sent directly to the Department of Justice, President Oaks did not argue, as DHEW had done several years earlier, that BYU was not telling landlords whom they could rent to, but was merely telling them that if they rented to members of the opposite sex they would take their approval away! His argument took a higher ground. President Oaks sought clarification of the relationship between the Fair Housing Act and Title IX because Title IX provided that separate hous-ing for men and women in on- and off-campus housing units did not consti-tute discrimination as long as the facilities were comparable. He also asked how the act intersected with BYU's First Amendment right to the free exercise of religion.

Representatives of the Atlanta regional office of the OCR attempted to enforce Title IX regulations against Louisburg College and Milligan College in 1974 before the regulations became effective. When this was pointed out to a DHEW representative several years later she replied that since the regulations had now been signed by the president and were in effect, the point was moot. When it was observed that the agency had violated the law by its actions nevertheless, the DHEW representative simply said, "Sue us, we haven't lost yet" (Gehring, personal communication, Sept. 9, 1975).

Bureaucratic aggressiveness was also evidenced when OCR attempted to exercise control over higher education's curriculum. Initially OCR included a section in Title IX regulations (§86.34[c]) requiring institutions to "establish and use internal procedures for *reviewing curricula,* designed both to ensure that they do not reflect discrimination on the basis of sex and to resolve com-plaints concerning allegations of such discrimination, *pursuant to procedural standards to be prescribed by the Director of the Office of Civil Rights (OCR)"* [final emphasis added]. Although there was reference to possible First Amendment intrusions, comments were invited including definitions of discriminatory con-tent in curricular materials! Thanks to the efforts of Stanford president Richard Lyman, who wrote Secretary Weinberger, the proposed rule was never included in the final regulations (Lyman, 1979). Where would higher education be if President Lyman had not complained?

OCR not only has been overly zealous and aggressive in writing regulations but also has begun to micromanage *how* institutions must comply with those regulations. OCR recently told the University of California at Santa Cruz that it had inappropriately resolved one of the ninety-one sexual assault cases during the three-year period 1991–93. The case involved a sexual assault in which the offending student was suspended from school for a year. OCR found this sanction to be inadequate and failed to demonstrate a commitment on the part of the institution to take "strong and effective measures to remedy sexual harassment and assault campus wide" (OCR letter to UC-SC cited in notice of "probable violation" at UC-SC, 1994).

Most recently the department of education issued a "Dear Colleague" letter (GEN-9–91–27, p. 20) in which it provided an interpretation of the requirements of the Campus Security Act pending distribution of final regulations. The letter defined campus security officers to include counselors and residence hall staff for purposes of reporting to the occurrences of serious crimes on campus. The sponsor of the bill, Congressman Bill Goodling, wrote Secretary of Education Lamar Alexander (B. Goodling, personal communication, Nov. 8, 1991) stating that "the issue of who is and is not responsible for reporting campus crimes was discussed during conference meetings with the Senate. It was agreed at that time that counselors and campus residence directors would not be required to report campus crimes—for the exact reasons outlined above." However, even in light of this clear statement of congressional intent, six months later the Department of Education issued proposed rules in which residence hall directors were included in the definition of campus security officials (57 Fed. Reg. 30833, July 10, 1992). As a result of a massive letter-writing campaign by many individuals in housing and student affairs, the final regulations no longer name residence directors specifically, but they define security officers to include anyone who has significant responsibility for campus activities but not counseling (59 Fed. Reg. 22314).

Title VI, Title IX, and Section 504 each prohibit discrimination "under any education program or activity receiving federal financial assistance." The DHEW, and, subsequently the Department of Education (DE), however, aggressively enforced those laws by extending their coverage beyond those programs and activities receiving federal financial assistance. The department defined a program or activity to be the entire institution where federal funds in any amount went to even one student. It thus broadened enforcement to every aspect of an institution regardless of whether that particular program received federal funding (see *Bob Jones v. Johnson*, 1974). A dangerous precedent was thus established by this overzealous enforcement. The federal government now controlled privately funded activities.

Several institutions, including many small, private, religiously affiliated colleges, challenged this aggressive enforcement in a series of court battles and they were successful in limiting federal control to areas of federal spending (*Bennett v. West Texas University*, 1981; *Rice v. President and Fellows of Harvard College*, 1981; *Haffer v. Temple University*, 1982; *University of Richmond v. Bell*,

1982; *Hillsdale College v. Department of Health Education and Welfare,* 1982). In 1984 the United States Supreme Court affirmed that Title IX only applied to the specific program or activity receiving federal funding. The case involved Grove City College, a small, private, religiously affiliated institution. The college received no federal funds whatsoever, but it did enroll students who received federal student aid in the form of Basic Economic Opportunity Grants (BEOG) directly from the government under the alternative disbursement system. The college refused to sign a federal certificate of compliance for Title IX. The college claimed that it did not discriminate on the basis of sex because of its moral and religious beliefs and not because it was prohibited from doing so by federal mandates. The Court held that Grove City was a recipient and therefore required to sign the compliance form but that there was "no persuasive evidence suggesting that Congress intended that the department's regulatory authority follow federally aided students from classroom to classroom, building to building or activity to activity" (*Grove City College v. Bell,* 1984, at 573).

Four years later, the Department of Education was given that authority by Congress with the passage of the Civil Rights Restoration Act of 1987 (P.L. 100–259). This law makes Title VI, Title IX, and Section 504 applicable to *every* aspect of any college that receives *any* federal funding, including that which goes directly to a student. This law sets a dangerous precedent by allowing the federal government to control all aspects of a private organization's activities when only one small segment of the organization receives federal financial assistance.

Federal laws are now written to cover all aspects of an institution's operations by stating that, as a condition of receiving federal funds or any other form of federal aid, institutions must take certain actions. Thus, higher education, having once accepted federal aid with a promise that the government would not exercise any supervision, direction, or control, finds itself in a position where the government is controlling not only programs and activities that receive federal dollars but also everything the institution does. Colleges are now required by federal law to discipline both students and employees who violate alcoholic beverage laws, they are directed to monitor off-campus behavior on private property, and they are told how to calculate retention rates (see, for example, 20 U.S.C. 1092[e] and [f]).

Again, it is not the principles of nondiscrimination or safety that are objectionable—Grove City College did not discriminate—but, for example, it is the "jeopardy in which the law places cherished values that causes alarm" (Hobbs, 1978a, p. 3). Our nation was founded on the rejection of governmental interference in private life, yet we now have a government that passes laws that are more intrusive into private life than the edicts of King George were. Indeed, if we apply the same principle used by Congress and DE to nonacademic life, if your house was built with a veterans' loan or financed with an FHA mortgage, the government could chose to mandate that you discipline your children, provide them written notice of state and federal alcoholic beverage laws, and not discriminate between them when it comes to taking out the trash! As the former president of SUNY at Buffalo has observed, "Frankly, any central government that can regulate the sexual composition of grammar school choirs can aspire to regulate everything" (Ketter, 1978, p. 69). The President of the United States had to intercede when DHEW attempted to stop mother-daughter and father-son banquets, and Senator Bayh, one of the sponsors of Title IX, had to create an amendment to the act when DHEW also attempted to declare Boys' State and Girls' State an unlawful form of sex discrimination (120 Cong. Rec. S-21567–8, Dec. 16, 1974).

Finn (1978) summarized the problem when he said, "The federal enforcers see themselves as merely carrying out the laws. With this dutifulness come potential hazards—overzealousness, single-mindedness, unevenness, unreasonableness, inattentiveness, capriciousness, sluggishness—but these are endemic to the regulatory mode" (p. 149).

Agency bureaucrats are overzealous and overly aggressive in enforcing their regulations, and the regulations show a lack of understanding of how colleges and universities operate. A study conducted for Exxon Education Foundation concluded that "bureaucrats write regulations for 'hierarchial management systems and not for horizontal collegial systems where authority is shared'" (Editorial Projects for Education, 1979, p. 27). More recently, the Department of Education has again evidenced its complete lack of understanding of colleges and even the students it is attempting to save. The discussion of the regulations to implement the Drug Free Schools and Communities Act of 1989 states, "While the phrase 'in writing' does not appear in the statute, the Secretary believes that in order to ensure that each student has access to and can refer to the required materials, they must be in writing" (55 Fed. Reg. 33595). Anyone who has ever worked with college students knows exactly what happens when mass printed material is provided to students. They certainly don't refer to it! Furthermore, "merely making the materials available for those who wish to take them does not satisfy the requirements of Public Law 101–226" (55 Fed. Reg. 33595). When a representative of DE was asked how a commuter institution with 22,000 students, over 95 percent of whom lived off-campus, could meet the requirement, the response was "hand it out at registration" (Gehring, personal communication, Sept. 1990). When was the last time you saw a college or university with over five thousand students have them register by standing in line? How many students do you know who "refer" to the DFSCAA information? If you spend the money to mail the information, what do you think students will do with it? Even after research provided to the DE showed that students know most of the mandated information before entering college and learn the least from the mailings after entering college, the DE refuses to change its regulations to be more in line with other federal rules that require only that information is provided "by any means that are reasonably likely to inform . . . students of their rights" [34 C.F.R. § 9.7(c)].

Economist Early Cheit has observed that typical bureaucrats "require the gathering of useless data; they cause long inexplicable delays; they play 'cat and mouse' games over enforcement; they conduct endless reviews. Sometimes after periods of indecision, the decisions they do make are uninformed about the educational process. It has apparently come as news to some GS-12s that a library is needed for research (cited in Editorial Projects for Education, 1979, p. 22).

Cheit's observation is supported by a former president of the University of Michigan. "The cost and effort [of compiling information] might be justified if it could be demonstrated that it is productive. On the contrary, it is evident that enforcement agencies are not staffed to examine and analyze the mountains of material which they are accumulating. Unless the whole procedure is a form of punishment . . . it is hard to see what really useful purpose it is serving" (*Hearings on Federal Higher Education Programs' Institutional Eligibility,* 1974).

Hall and Donnell (1985), who coined the term "bureaupathic," have studied government managers and provide a possible explanation for the hostile relationship with higher education that has arisen. The bureaupathic management style is found to be prevalent in government. Bureaupathic managers "pressure otherwise normal and healthy subordinates to behave in pathological ways" (p. 40). These managers espouse Theory X styles of management significantly more often than their private sector counterparts. The authors say government bureaucrats "operate from a pessimistic and reductive view of the human resources available to them and eschew both the concerns of production and people in favor of procedure and precedent" (p. 43).

This sentiment is echoed by the former president of the State University of New York at Buffalo who, in referring to the effect of the plethora of regulations, said, "Procedures become more important than the quality of human relationships" (Ketter, 1978, p. 67).

Other Costs

Justice Scalia (1978) has characterized federal regulation of higher education as "regulation by munificence," in which the government turns funds meant as a carrot to accomplish one end into a stick to compel submission toward another. Higher education is beginning to understand that the carrot is not that sweet and that the cost of compliance may outweigh the benefit of the federal financial assistance.

An early study by the American Council on Education (ACE) concluded that in 1976 the cost of compliance was somewhere between 1 and 4 percent of an institution's total operating budget (Van Alstyne and Coldren, 1975). A year earlier it was estimated that the total cost to higher education of complying with federally mandated programs was equal to the total of all voluntary contributions to higher education ("Will Government Patronage Kill the Universities?" 1975). In 1978 Finn said, "Rarely does the money offset the cost of complying with such regulations" (p. 148). These estimates were made before implementation of yet additional laws and regulations, which there has been no funding to help carry out, and during a time when higher education has experienced massive budget cuts. Today's cost of compliance is most likely much higher.

Financial costs, as debilitating as they are, cannot, however, compare with the "deadening monotony" induced by federal regulations (Nobles, 1978, p. 22). Political science professor Paul Seabury (1979a) predicted an "obliteration of 'distinctions among institutions' " (p. 23). He said, "Thus, as federal directives governing university policies multiply in meticulous detail, they apply equally to all affected institutions. Clearly, considering the federal government's desire to evenhandedly pursue its social goals through institutions of higher learning, one effect of this is to gradually or even spasmodically obliterate the dynamic diversity of higher education in the United States" (Seabury, 1979a, p. 23)

Maybe this is why institutions have recently been directed to define their unique niche in the market through strategic planning strategies.

What Can Be Done?

It is clear that the problem is very serious. Institutions were told that if they accepted federal funds, they would not be controlled. In their financial need, institutions accepted funds only to find, as the addict did who was first given free drugs, that once they were dependent, the price skyrocketed. An adversarial relationship has developed, and there has been a loss of trust. And the federal government owns postsecondary education now. As Kingman Brewster, the former president of Yale University, has observed, the government believes that because it bought the button, it has a right to design the coat (cited in Finn, 1978). If any federal funds flow to any part of the institution, every activity of an institution is covered by federal laws and regulations regardless of whether the activity is federally or privately funded. Few distinctions between public and private institutions now exist, because almost all private institutions receive federal funding in some form or another. What the Constitution does not require of private organizations, Congress may, by mandating it for recipients of federal financial assistance. Federal legislators have already attempted to impose First Amendment restrictions on private organizations (Freedom of Speech on Campus Act of 1991, S. 1484, and Collegiate Speech Protection Act of 1991, H.R. 1380). Higher education has lost its diversity and has become homogenized. The "federal university," proposed by Charles Pickney of South Carolina in 1787, has now become reality without even a congressional vote.

We in higher education must reclaim our institutions and protect our liberties from those "men of zeal; well meaning but without understanding." There are a variety of ways to do this. In the late 1970s, when administrators were so vociferous in their lament over federal regulations, self-regulation was seen as the panacea. Frankly, I have little faith that self-regulation, although necessary for a collegial institution, will keep the wolf from the door. Recall that most institutions were providing access to student records and generally not releasing them to unauthorized persons years before the Buckley amendment was thrust upon us. And long before the Drug Free Schools and Communities Act Amendments were passed, colleges and universities were confronting the drug and alcohol problem with peer education, organizations like BACCHUS and SADD, national conferences, and special weeks of programming dedicated to teaching students about the problems associated with alcohol and drugs. If we are to reclaim our institutions, we must do more.

John Gardner (1990), a former secretary of HEW, has observed that the key to leadership is trust. If the federal government has ever had the capacity to provide leadership to higher education, it has lost it. Higher education can no longer trust government. This is a truly sad situation, but it must be recognized if higher education is to move forward unfettered by federal control. To be sure, some of this loss of trust between the two parties has evolved because of higher education's own intransigence, but the government's cure has been worse than the disease. Institutions and individual administrators must be much more proactive and reclaim control of our institutions to ensure that we do not lose the diversity and freedom of institutional discretion that have made this nation's public and private institutions of higher education the envy of the world.

A recommended proactive strategy is for campus administrators to stay abreast of proposed laws and rules and to respond to them. In Chapter Five Schuh and Ogle discuss resources that can help keep administrators current. Once it has been determined that legislation or rules are being proposed, administrators must respond to the appropriate agency or congressperson with thoughtful reactions. Higher education administrators have not responded very often in the past to DE or OCR proposed rule making and probably less frequently to legislators.

Professional associations must also accept some responsibility for responding to proposed legislation and rules. Higher education has been seen in the past as unable to present a united front and has been criticized for "an overabundance of rhetoric and an underabundance of fact" (Ketter, 1978, p. 68). Professional associations must do a better job of informing their constituents of new legislation and proposed rules and develop position papers on the effect these laws and regulations have on members and their institutions. In order to respond effectively, associations must do a much better job of knowing their membership and having good data upon which they can formulate reasoned and convincing responses.

Administrators must also maintain regular contact with federal legislators and their staffs. Frequent interaction when there are no major bills pending or no problems with federal rules will help establish a relationship. We must let our congressional representatives know what's happening on campus—"layer" them with information on a regular basis. This will give them the ammunition they need to counter legislation regulating the campus.

A more radical strategy is to bring suit to have the Civil Rights Restoration Act of 1987 declared unconstitutional. In speaking to the Fellows of the American Bar Association Foundation, former Yale University president Kingman Brewster (1975) said:

> It is not sufficient to say that since the government is paying the bills, therefore it has a right to specify the product. This would be understandable if all that is being offered were special support for the program of special federal interest. To say, however, that support for all general educational activities of national importance will be withheld unless a school enlarges the program the government is interested in, is to use the threat of cutting off aid for one purpose in order to accomplish another . . . . This is constitutionally objectionable, even in the name of a good cause [cited in 121 Cong. Rec. 5, 1975 at 5828].

Brewster's remarks were directed at OCR's aggressive application of the "infection theory," which holds that the receipt of a federal dollar in one area subjects the entire institution to regulation. The Supreme Court agreed with Brewster and rejected HEW's theory in *Grove City College v. Bell.* His remarks are equally applicable to the Civil Rights Restoration Act, which Congress passed after *Bell* and now has the same effect. Courts determine the constitutionality of legislation. As yet, no one has challenged either the Civil Rights Restoration Act or the authority of Congress to pass laws mandating that institutions develop programs and provide information to all students if they have but one who is receiving federal aid. How do they derive the right to design the coat when they bought only the button? We must challenge that assertion.

Let there be no mistake: this challenge would not be designed to encourage institutions to halt their progress in eliminating discrimination, drug use, crime, or fraud. Rather it would be for the purpose of halting a very dangerous precedent, which allows the government to infringe upon privately financed programs and activities. There is a higher moral ground that institutions must take in eliminating discrimination, drugs, and crime and in dealing fairly with students. Institutions like Grove City College have made that argument. They have ascended to those heights without being told they must do so by the government.

Higher education has been too polite in the past and has been "reluctant to resort to formal procedures and lawsuits" (Gellhorn and Boyer, 1978, p. 44). Institutions must recognize that the federal government's mandates must be challenged in court—as one adversary to the other.

Whether higher education is successful in challenging congressional authority to control every aspect of an institution or not, administrators must be much more proactive in asserting the rights of the institution. More institutions must risk giving up federal financial assistance. A crazy idea? In 1977 "fourteen universities decided to forfeit $11 million in fiscal 1978 capetation grants rather than comply" with a provision of the health manpower legislation that would have required medical schools to admit into the third-year class medical students who had studied two years abroad and without regard to "requirements related to academic qualifications" (Finn, 1978, p. 152). The government withdrew the admission qualification portion of the requirement after the institutions decided to forfeit the funds.

Summary

The diversity in higher education in this country has made our system one of the best in the world. That diversity is now threatened by federal intervention into the very way in which our institutions are administered. Higher education is becoming the federal university, with Congress and the regulatory agencies its trustees; however, the government is exercising the kind of control over our institutions that even local trustees would not consider.

The government's goals in directing higher education have been beneficent. They would be acceptable if left to the institutions to accomplish, and I believe our institutions would have accomplished them. Admittedly, higher education is slow to change, but in that respect it mirrors society. Institutions committed to seeking the truth are purposefully slow to embrace change. However, those who argue that higher education would change only if regulated place too much stock in law as a panacea. They condemn our colleges and universities as incapable of seeking the truth and the inherent goodness embodied in truth.

Aleksandr Solzhenitsyn (1978) described our situation when he wrote:

> I have spent all my life under a communist regime and I tell you that a society without any objective legal scale is a terrible one indeed. But a society with no other scale but the legal one is not quite worthy of man either. A society which is based on the letter of the law and never reaches any higher is taking very scarce advantage of the high level of human possibilities. The letter of the law is too cold and formal to have a beneficial influence on society. Whenever the tissue of life is woven of legalistic relations, there is an atmosphere of moral mediocrity, paralyzing man's noblest impulses [p. B1].

We must not allow the government to reduce our institutions to moral mediocrity and thereby paralyze our noblest impulses. We must regain our institutions and take advantage of the highest level of human and institutional potential.

References

Advisory Commission on Intergovernmental Relations. "The Federal Role in the Federal System: The Dynamics of Growth." Commission Report. Washington, D.C.: Advisory Commission on Intergovernmental Relations, 1981.

Bailey, S. K. "The Peculiar Mixture: Public Norms and Private Space." In W. C. Hobbs (ed.), *Government Regulation of Higher Education*. Cambridge, Mass.: Ballinger, 1978.

Bennett, R. K. "Colleges Under the Federal Gun." *Reader's Digest,* 1976, *108*(649), 126–130.

Brewster, K. Address to the Fellows of the American Bar Association, Feb. 22, 1975. In 121 Congressional Record 5827 (daily ed. Mar. 10, 1975).

Brubacher, J. S., and Rudy, W. *Higher Education in Transition: A History of American Colleges and Universities, 1936–1968.* New York: HarperCollins, 1968.

DeLoughry, T. J. "Bennett Says Colleges Aren't Doing Enough in War on Drugs." *Chronicle of Higher Education,* 1989, *35*(42), A18.

Dutton, T. B., Smith, F. W., and Zarle, T. *Institutional Approaches to the Adjudication of Student Misconduct.* Monograph No. 2. Washington, D.C.: National Association of Student Personnel Administrators Division of Research and Publications, 1969.

Editorial Projects for Education. "The Entangling Web: Federal Regulation of Colleges and Universities." *Georgia Alumni Record,* 1979, *58*(5), 17–32.

Edwards, H. T. *Higher Education and the Unholy Crusade Against Governmental Regulation.* Cambridge, Mass.: Harvard University Institute for Educational Management, 1980.

Finn, C. E. *Scholars, Dollars, and Bureaucrats.* Washington, D.C.: The Brookings Institute, 1978.

Fishbein, E. A. "The Academic Industry—A Dangerous Premise." In W. C. Hobbs (ed.), *Government Regulation of Higher Education*. Cambridge, Mass.: Ballinger, 1978.

Fleming, R. W. "Who Will Be Regulated, and Why?" In W. C. Hobbs (ed.), *Government Regulation of Higher Education*. Cambridge, Mass.: Ballinger, 1978.

Gardner, J. *On Leadership.* New York: Free Press, 1990.

Gellhorn, E., and Boyer, B. B. "The Academy as a Regulated Industry." In W. C. Hobbs (ed.), *Government Regulation of Higher Education*. Cambridge, Mass.: Ballinger, 1978.

Gladieux, L. E., and Lewis, G. L. *The Federal Government and Higher Education: Traditions, Trends, Stakes, and Issues.* New York: College Entrance Examination Board, 1987.

Hall, J., and Donnell, S. M. "The Quiet Crisis in Government." *The Bureaucrat,* 1985, *14*(2), 39–44.

Hearings on Federal Higher Education Programs' Institutional Eligibility. 93rd Congress, 2nd session, 1974, pt. 2A, 93–94.

Hobbs, W. C. (ed.). *Government Regulation of Higher Education*. Cambridge, Mass.: Ballinger, 1978a.

Hobbs, W. C. "The Theory of Government Regulation." In W. C. Hobbs (ed.), *Government Regulation of Higher Education*. Cambridge, Mass.: Ballinger, 1978b.

Ketter, R. L. "By Hemp or by Silk, the Outcome Is the Same." In W. C. Hobbs (ed.), *Government Regulation of Higher Education*. Cambridge, Mass.: Ballinger, 1978.

Lyman, R. W. "Federal Regulation and Institutional Autonomy: A University President's View." In P. Seabury (ed.), *Bureaucrats and Brainpower: Government Regulation of Universities*. San Francisco: Institute for Contemporary Studies, 1979.

Moynihan, D. P. "The Politics of Higher Education." *Daedelus,* 1975, *104,* 128–147.

Nobles, L. "Facing the Government/Church-relatedness Issue." *The Southern Baptist Educator,* 1978, *62*(6), 22–28.

Palmer, C. J., Gehring, D. D., and Guthrie, V. L. "Student Knowledge of Information Mandated by the 1989 Amendments to the Drug Free Schools and Communities Act." *NASPA Journal,* 1992, *30*(1), 30–42.

Rainsford, G. N. *Congress and Higher Education in the Nineteenth Century.* Knoxville: The University of Tennessee Press, 1972.

Ross, D. *Preparing for Ulysses: Politics and Veterans During World War II.* New York: Columbia University Press, 1969.

Rudolph, F. *The American College and University: A History.* Athens: University of Georgia Press, 1990.

Scalia, A. "Guadalajara! A Case Study in Regulation by Munificence." *Regulation,* 1978, *2,* 23–29.

Seabury, P. "The Advent of the Academic Bureaucrats." In P. Seabury (ed.), *Bureaucrats and Brainpower: Government Regulation of Universities.* San Francisco: Institute for Contemporary Studies, 1979a.

Seabury, P. (ed.). *Bureaucrats and Brainpower: Government Regulation of Universities.* San Francisco: Institute for Contemporary Studies, 1979b.

"Senate Approves Higher Vocational Education Bill." *Higher Education and National Affairs,* Aug. 27, 1976, 25(33), p. 1.

Solzhenitsyn, A. "Why the West Has Succumbed to Cowardice." *Montreal Star, News and Review,* June 10, 1978.

Sumberg, A. D. "The Impact of Government Regulation on the Academic Occupation." In W. C. Hobbs (ed.), *Government Regulation of Higher Education.* Cambridge, Mass.: Ballinger, 1978.

Van Alstyne, C., and Coldren, S. "The Costs of Implementing Federally Mandated Social Programs at Colleges and Universities." Special report. Washington, D.C.: American Council on Education, 1975.

Weinberger, C. W. "Regulating the Universities." In P. Seabury (ed.), *Bureaucrats and Brainpower: Government Regulation of Universities.* San Francisco: Institute for Contemporary Studies, 1979.

"Will Government Patronage Kill the Universities?" Editorial. *Change,* 1975, 7(10), 10–12, 60–61.

Williams, R. L. *The Origins of Federal Support for Higher Education.* University Park: Pennsylvania State University Press, 1991.

Wilson, J. T. *Academic Science, Higher Education, and the Federal Government, 1950–1983.* Chicago: University of Chicago Press, 1983.

Winkler, K. J. "U.S. Officials Promise Colleges Relief from Government Rules." *Chronicle of Higher Education,* 1981, 22(20), 1, 8.

Cases

Bennett v. West Texas University, 799 F.2d 155 (5th Cir. 1981).

Bob Jones v. Johnson, 396 F.Supp. 597 (D. S.C. Greenville Div. 1974).

Grove City College v. Bell, 465 U.S. 555 (1984).

Haffer v. Temple University, 688 F.2d 14 (3rd Cir. 1982).

Hillsdale College v. Department of Health Education and Welfare, 696 F.2d 418 (6th Cir. 1982).

Olmstead v. United States, 277 U.S. 438 (1927).

Red and Black Publishing Company, Inc. v. Board of Regents, 427 S.E. 2d 257 (Ga. 1993).

Rice v. President and Fellows of Harvard College, 663 F.2d 336 (1st Cir. 1981).

The Shreveport Professional Chapter of the Society of Professional Journalists v. Louisiana State University Shreveport, case #393,333 (1st Jud. Ct., Caddo Parish, La. 1994).

University of Richmond v. Bell, 543 F.Supp. 321 (E.D. Va., Richmond Div. 1982).

DONALD D. GEHRING *is professor of higher education and student affairs and director of the higher education doctoral program at Bowling Green State University.*

This chapter offers a selection of annotated resources that will be helpful to student affairs practitioners as they seek to learn more about the policy process and continue to monitor federal interventions into campus affairs.

Selected Resources on Federal Policy and Student Affairs

Michael D. Coomes, Donald D. Gehring

Student affairs practice has a long tradition of borrowing from a variety of disciplines to form its knowledge base. Our theories of student development draw upon research done in psychology, sociology, and anthropology. In the same way, our understanding of policy and the impact policy has on the provision of services to students must draw upon a wide range of disciplinary sources, including political science, public administration, law, and policy studies. Therefore, this section will offer few resources drawn explicitly from student affairs practice (the one exception is the area of student financial aid, perhaps the student affairs area with the closest ties to the federal policy arena). Rather, it will present policy resources that will be useful to student affairs practitioners as they seek to understand the policy process and the outcomes of federal intervention.

Policy Analyses and Case Studies

Eaton, J. S. *The Unfinished Agenda: Higher Education and the 1980s.* New York: Macmillan, 1991.
     This is an extensive examination of the political and policy climate during the Reagan years. The book addresses three fundamental questions: (1) What were the important issues to the higher education community during the 1980s? (2) How effectively did the community accomplish those goals? and (3) What still needs to be done as higher education moves into the 1990s? This book differs from other case studies in that it takes a wider view, focusing

on a range of policy areas including academic and curricular reform, student aid, and access and choice issues.

Gladieux, L. E., and Wolanin, T. R. *Congress and the Colleges.* Lexington, Mass.: Lexington Books, 1976.

A classic in student affairs policy analysis, this is an exhaustive study of the substantive and procedural factors that led to the passage of the Education Amendments of 1972. Part historical narrative and part policy analysis, the book provides valuable insight into how higher education legislation is developed. The authors conclude their analysis with an excellent discussion of the higher education policy arena and with observations about the process that results in the formulation of higher education policy.

McPherson, M. S., and Schapiro, M. O. *Keeping College Affordable: Government and Educational Opportunity.* Washington, D.C.: Brookings Institute, 1991.

This is a comprehensive exploration of the role student financial aid has played in fostering equity and access. The authors use a range of historical and econometric lenses to examine the impact of federal student aid on college financing, enrollment, and student access and choice. The authors conclude their discussion with suggestions for improving public policy for higher education finance.

Wilson, J. T. *Academic Science, Higher Education, and the Federal Government, 1950–1983.* Chicago: University of Chicago Press, 1983.

This compact volume provides a perspective on federal policy as it relates to academic science in higher education. The volume presents a historical analysis of the relationship between federal policy and higher education, particularly in the sciences, from the end of World War II through the Reagan administration.

Merisotis, J. P. (ed.). *The Changing Dimensions of Student Aid.* New Directions for Higher Education, no. 74. San Francisco: Jossey-Bass, 1991.

This is an examination of the need for changes in the student aid system. The sourcebook examines the roles that students and parents play in financing higher education, federal-state-institutional policy coordination, the complex and little-understood student aid delivery system, the role of the student aid office, and how student aid policy can be developed to enhance student persistence in college.

The Policy Process and Policy Analysis

The following resources provide insight into the policy-making process and offer models for conducting policy analysis and evaluation. These resources supplement the materials discussed in Chapter Two.

Brewer, G., and DeLeon, P. *The Foundations of Policy Analysis.* Homewood, Ill.: Dorsey Press, 1983.

In this comprehensive overview of the policy process, the authors trace the process of policy development through six stages: initiation, estimation, selection, implementation, evaluation, and termination. Each stage is explained in depth, and, where appropriate, multiple models and approaches are offered.

Kelman, S. *Making Public Policy: A Hopeful View of American Government.* New York: Basic Books, 1987.

This book is both an explanation and critique of the current federal policy process. The author provides two analytical frameworks: (1) politics, with its emphasis on policy formulation, and (2) production, with its emphasis on implementation. The author also examines a variety of institutional settings that shape and implement policy, including Congress, bureaucratic agencies, the Supreme Court, and the civil service. The book concludes with an analysis of government effectiveness.

Nachmias, D. *Public Policy Evaluation: Approaches and Methods.* New York: St. Martin's Press, 1979.

This is a guidebook for conducting quantitative policy studies. A variety of analytical approaches, including policy experimentation, quasi experimentation, regression analyses, and structural equation models, are presented. The author also provides a brief discussion of why policy evaluation is needed.

Pavela, G. *SYNFAX.* Crofton, Md.: Synfax, Inc.

This is a three-page fax published weekly that covers a variety of policy and legal topics culled from current newspapers, journals, magazines, and other sources. It discusses the implications of these topics for practice. An excellent source for keeping up with the most current events affecting higher education.

Ripley, R. B., and Franklin, G. A. *Policy Implementation and Bureaucracy.* (2nd ed.) Chicago: Dorsey Press, 1986.

This is an introduction to the concept of implementation, or "what happens after a bill becomes a law" (p. v). In addition to discussing the general concept of policy implementation, the authors discuss the relationship between implementation and policy types (for example, distributive, competitive regulatory, protective regulatory, and redistributive). Extensive examples of the implementation of each type of policy are drawn from a wider range of policy arenas (for example, public housing, maritime industries). The book also offers an extensive discussion of the politics of implementation.

Williams, W., and others. *Studying Implementation: Methodological and Administrative Issues.* Chatham, N.J.: Chatham House, 1982.

This useful sourcebook provides valuable insight into methodological issues related to the study of the implementation of public policy. Methodological issues addressed include field network evaluation studies, longitudinal approaches, and data collection techniques (for example, participant observation). The chapter on backwards mapping as a technique for studying the policy process is particularly helpful. The book includes a case study of Title I of the Elementary and Secondary Education Act.

Wise, C. R. *The Dynamic of Legislation: Leadership and Policy Change in the Congressional Process.* San Francisco: Jossey-Bass, 1991.
    This is an extensive and trenchant discussion of how Congress works (and sometimes fails to work effectively). After answering the controversial question "Can Congress legislate to meet today's challenges?" the author addresses such issues as policy initiation, congressional agenda setting, consensus building, and overcoming opposition. The procedural dimensions of congressional policy making are explored through an examination of how Congress has grappled with a variety of crime control measures, including the Comprehensive Crime Control Act.

Legal Resources

Kaplin, W. A. *The Law of Higher Education.* (2nd ed.) San Francisco: Jossey-Bass, 1985.
    This is an excellent text on higher education law that includes separate sections on students, federal laws and regulations, and staff issues.

Bickel, R. *College Administrators and the Courts.* Asheville, N.C.: College Administration Publications, 1988.
    These are briefs of the major court cases involving the relationship between faculty, staff, and their colleges. Title VII cases are extensively covered.

Pavela, G. *Synthesis: Law and Policy in Higher Education.* Asheville, N.C.: College Administration Publications.
    This bimonthly publication focuses on a specific topic of concern to student affairs administrators. Includes interviews with noted experts and synthesizes the law applicable to the topic.

National Association of Student Personnel Administrators. *NASPA Forum.*
    This is a newsletter of the association. It contains columns on new federal legislation and how it affects student affairs. The regular column "Abreast of the Law" includes comments on federal laws and regulations as well as court cases of interest to student affairs practitioners.

Palmer, C. J., and Gehring, D. D. (eds.). *A Handbook for Complying with the Program and Review Requirements of the 1989 Amendments to the Drug*

Free Schools and Communities Act. Asheville, N.C.: College Administration Publications, 1992.

This useful handbook contains chapters on the requirements of the law, research implications, resources for funding and prevention, and how to conduct a biennial review. The appendixes include a copy of the final regulations and responses by the Department of Education, CAS standards, the CORE survey, and other assessment instruments as well as a list of FIPSE network schools.

Young, P. D., and Gehring, D. *College Students and the Courts.* Asheville, N.C.: College Administration Publications, 1986.

Briefs of selected court cases affecting the student/institutional relationship. Contains selected federal laws and regulations.

Legislative Resources

A number of publications provide regular updates on legislative action. Both the *Chronicle of Higher Education* and *Education Daily* provide in-depth, regular coverage of the "Washington scene." This section will provide additional information on resources that may already be available on most college campuses. Student affairs administrators are encouraged to contact their governmental relations office, president's office, and fellow administrators to secure access to these resources.

American Council on Education. *Higher Education and National Affairs.*

This is a regular publication of the association that includes short articles on a variety of topics of interest to administrators. The government relations office of ACE monitors federal laws and regulations and alerts readers to new issues in the publication.

Congressional Quarterly Services. *Congressional Quarterly Weekly Report* and *Congressional Quarterly Almanac.* Washington, D.C.: Congressional Quarterly Services.

The *Congressional Quarterly Weekly Report* is perhaps the most comprehensive and current resource on legislative action. The *Weekly Report* provides extensive discussion of major legislation, executive branch policy initiatives, congressional voting records, and background information on policy issues. The *Congressional Quarterly Almanac* summarizes the legislative action of the preceding year. Each almanac contains a section focusing on education legislation.

National Association of Student Financial Aid Administrators. *NASFAA Newsletter* and *Federal Monitor.* Washington, D.C.: National Association of Student Financial Aid Administrators.

The *NASFAA Newsletter* is produced bimonthly and contains extensive discussion of legislative and regulatory issues facing financial aid offices.

Because many other federal mandates (for example, compliance with Title IX and the provisions of FERPA) are tied to institutional receipt of federal student aid funds, the *NASFAA Newsletter* contains valuable information on related legislation and regulation. A very timely and current resource and an excellent source of information on various proposals under consideration as Congress reauthorizes the Higher Education Act of 1965 every five years. The *NASFAA Federal Monitor* reprints both proposed and final rules contained in Federal Register that impact the operation of the federal student aid programs. Financial aid offices of institutional members of the National Association of Student Financial Aid Administrators receive copies of both the *NASFAA Newsletter* and *Federal Monitor.*

MICHAEL D. COOMES *is assistant professor of higher education and student affairs at Bowling Green State University.*

DONALD D. GEHRING *is professor of higher education and student affairs and director of the higher education doctoral program at Bowling Green State University.*

APPENDIX

Primary Federal Laws and Regulations Affecting Student Affairs Practices in Higher Education

Statute	Public Law Number or Location in U.S. Code	Applicable Regulations Appear at:	General Direction
Title VI of the Civil Rights Act of 1964	42 U.S.C. § 2000d et seq.	34 C.F.R. 100	Prohibits discrimination on the basis of race, color, or national origin in educational programs receiving federal financial assistance (FFA).
Title VII of the Civil Rights Act of 1964	42 U.S.C. § 2000e et seq.	29 C.F.R. 1602	Prohibits discrimination on the basis of race, color, or national origin, sex, and religion (with some exceptions) *in employment.*
Title IX of the Education Amendments of 1972	20 U.S.C. § 1681	34 C.F.R. 106	Prohibits discrimination on the basis of sex in educational programs and activities receiving FFA.
Section 504 of the Rehabilitation Act of 1973	29 U.S.C. § 749	34 C.F.R. 104	Prohibits discrimination against otherwise qualified handicapped individuals in educational programs and activities receiving FFA.
Family Educational Rights and Privacy Act of 1974	20 U.S.C. § 1232	34 C.F.R. 99	Provides students access to their records (with exceptions) and prohibits disclosure without consent (with exceptions).
Institutional and Financial Assistance for Students (Consumer Information Act)	20 U.S.C. § 1092	34 C.F.R. 668.41	Information to be provided to all current and prospective students by institutions that participate in any financial aid program under Title IV of the Higher Education Act of 1965 (federal student aid).
Student Right-to-Know and Campus Security Act (includes the Sexual Assault Victim's Bill)	Amends 20 U.S.C. § 1092	59 Fed. Reg. 22314 (Apr. 29, 1994)	Requires additional information on graduation and campus crime rates as well as mandating anti-crime programs for institutions receiving federal student aid.

(continued)

Statute	Public Law Number or Location in U.S. Code	Applicable Regulations Appear at:	General Direction
Drug Free Schools and Communities Act and Amendments of 1989	20 U.S.C. § 1145	34 C.F.R. 86	Mandates information that must be provided to students and employees concerning the possession and use of illicit drugs and underage alcohol consumption. Also requires institutions to discipline students and employees for violations.
Americans with Disabilities Act of 1990	42 U.S.C. § 12101 et seq.		Prohibits discrimination against qualified individuals with a disability. Applies to both public and private sector transportation, communication, programs, and facilities. Very comprehensive.
Higher Education Act of 1965	17 U.S.C. § 101 et seq.		Most comprehensive law affecting higher education. Includes sections on libraries, faculty development, international and Indian education graduate programs, facilities, and student financial aid.
Copyright Revision Act of 1976	17 U.S.C. § 101 et seq.		Provides for the protection of copyrighted works and includes definitions and fair use standards.
Fair Labor Standards Act of 1938 as amended	29 U.S.C. § 201 et seq.	There are 28 different sets of regulations stemming from this law.	Designed to eliminate labor conditions detrimental to the health, efficiency, and well-being of employees, including domestic service workers. Sets forth minimum wage and hour standards.

INDEX

ORDERING INFORMATION

NEW DIRECTIONS FOR STUDENT SERVICES is a series of paperback books that offers guidelines and programs for aiding students in their total development—emotional, social, and physical, as well as intellectual. Books in the series are published quarterly in spring, summer, fall, and winter and are available for purchase by subscription as well as by single copy.

SUBSCRIPTIONS for 1994 cost $47.00 for individuals (a savings of 25 percent over single-copy prices) and $62.00 for institutions, agencies, and libraries. Please do not send institutional checks for personal subscriptions. Standing orders are accepted.

SINGLE COPIES cost $15.95 when payment accompanies order. (California, New Jersey, New York, and Washington, D.C., residents please include appropriate sales tax.) Billed orders will be charged postage and handling.

DISCOUNTS FOR QUANTITY ORDERS are available. Please write to the address below for information.

ALL ORDERS must include either the name of an individual or an official purchase order number. Please submit your order as follows:
   Subscriptions: specify series and year subscription is to begin
   Single copies: include individual title code (such as SS55)

MAIL ALL ORDERS TO:
   Jossey-Bass Publishers
   350 Sansome Street
   San Francisco, California 94104-1342

FOR SUBSCRIPTION SALES OUTSIDE OF THE UNITED STATES, CONTACT:
   any international subscription agency or Jossey-Bass directly.